Robert Duvall

Robert Duvall

HOLLYWOOD MAVERICK

Judith Slawson

St. Martin's Press
New York

ROBERT DUVALL. Copyright © 1985 by Judith Slawson. All rights reserved. Printed in the United States of America. No part of this book may be used or reproduced in any manner whatsoever without written permission except in the case of brief quotations embodied in critical articles or reviews. For information, address St. Martin's Press, 175 Fifth Avenue, New York, N.Y. 10010.

Design by Paolo Pepe

Library of Congress Cataloging in Publication Data

Slawson, Judith.
    Robert Duvall : Hollywood maverick.

    1. Duvall, Robert.   2. Actors—United States—
Biography.   I. Title.
PN2287.D88S53   1985   792'.028'0924 [B]   85-11794
ISBN 0-312-68708-7

First Edition

10 9 8 7 6 5 4 3 2 1

For Dennis Lucchesi,
who shows me how to slay the dragons.

Contents

Acknowledgments

I wish to thank the staff of the Billy Rose Theatre Collection at the New York Public Library and the Museum of the Performing Arts for their assistance in researching the material for this book.

1

A NAVY BRAT
MASTERS MIMICRY

Robert Duvall is not a movie star glittering brightly in the
celebrity firmament. His is the luminous glow of a rare talent nurtured through long years of perfecting a craft; he is
an actor who didn't use Hollywood hype to promote his career. No glitzy media-made image has wedged itself between Duvall's audience and the role he's playing. His
performances have been so convincing that for a long time
the actor has remained faceless while the characters he has
portrayed have taken on a life of their own in the popular
imagination.

When it finally dawned on the public that such diverse
roles as the ultracompetent *consigliere* in *The Godfather,* the
brawling Marine fighter pilot in *The Great Santini,* and the
down-and-out country and western singer in *Tender Mercies*
were played by the same actor, Duvall had won an Oscar for
the latter part. Then came the flash of recognition. Wasn't
he the one who played Dr. Watson, Jesse James, Ike? And
so on, all the way back through twenty years and thirty-
three films in which Duvall seemed so totally to encompass
the parts he played that his own identity got lost in the shuf-
fle of images from dirt farmers to Nazi officers.

The Oscar Duvall won for the leading role of Mac Sledge
in *Tender Mercies* was not the icing on the cake of a splashy
success story. It was Hollywood's tribute to a most hard-
working and unassuming maverick. It was the proof too

rarely seen that artistic integrity *can* pay off when it's backed by extraordinary talent and a gritty commitment to the quest for perfection.

The roots of that quest sink deep into the soil of traditional American values, typified by the actor's father, William Howard Duvall, a Virginian of French Huguenot descent affectionately called "Willy" by his three sons. A naval officer, he entered Annapolis at sixteen and worked his way up through the ranks, making captain at thirty-nine and retiring as a rear admiral. His career was the focus of the family's life because they followed where it led him. Robert, always known as "Bodge" to his family, was born in San Diego in 1931. His parents didn't stay there long, however, soon moving to the East Coast, where they lived in a number of port cities, primarily Annapolis.

These travels instilled in the future actor a keen sense of the rich diversity of accents, speech patterns, and mannerisms that gives American regional life its zesty flavor. Highly impressionable, he was quick to pick up on personal quirks. When he was four years old, Bodge sat at the crowded dinner table of his uncle's Idaho ranch and imitated a lonely old sheepherder vigorously attacking his food while the assembled cowboys laughed uproariously and his mother cringed with embarrassment.

A confluence of circumstances gave Robert Duvall an early access to a wide sampling of local dialects and cultures; his native curiosity and gift of mimicry put that exposure to good use. His father's family came from Lorton, Virginia, an area south of Alexandria that was in those days not yet suburban, but still retained its old-fashioned country flavor. His mother's East Texas background gave him a knowledge of southwestern traditions, while the boyhood summers spent on her sister's Montana ranch rounded off this immersion in rural Americana with a northwestern influence.

Duvall's feel for the nuances of rural American life, then, have the authenticity of childhood memories.

Besides the affinity for regional traditions and regional characteristics, another very strong influence on the young Duvall was religion. William and Mildred Duvall were both devout Christian Scientists. Christian Science is not a religion that can be practiced simply by a perfunctory church attendance; its basic tenet that faith in God can cure disease is one that must permeate the daily lives of those who embrace it. The kind of faith its adherents believe can heal all the ills to which flesh is heir is one that must be lived fully and fervently.

While Robert Duvall has rarely talked about his religious convictions, they do run deep in this man who, despite the influences of New York and Hollywood, neither smokes nor drinks. Not only does he never use recreational drugs, he avoids prescription ones, and visits to doctors as well. The mentality that says faith can cure is one that instills a sense of self-reliance and a capacity for discipline in a child, qualities that have characterized Duvall's career.

Regional distinctions and religious faith made their indelible marks on the highly observant boy, as did the military life-style. During World War II Rear Admiral Duvall was away in the North Atlantic ushering convoys of munition vessels, while his wife and sons lived in Annapolis. The lively Duvall boys must have been quite a handful, but Mildred Duvall was a solid Navy wife, strong and resilient, keeping things in order. Once a college drama major, she could appreciate her middle son's mimicry as well as the musical talent he shared with his older brother, William, nicknamed "Bud," and his younger one, John, called "Jack." Their mother encouraged the boisterous performances the boys put on at home and was warmly supportive of their interest in music.

Wartime Annapolis was an exciting place in which to grow up, and among the naval officers he met there Bodge must have seen plenty of prototypes for the military men he would so adroitly portray. Beside observing the fast-paced life around him, Bodge was as fascinated by the silver screen as any imaginative boy in those pre-TV days. He'd sit in the darkened theater captivated by the cliff-hanger serials. But his favorite movie was *Gunga Din:* "I dug Din . . . Sam Jaffe's part, the humble waterboy who in the end proves the bravest of them all." Even then, it was the more subtle role, the more complex, paradoxical character to which he was most drawn.

Bodge was not as enchanted with his schoolwork as he was with movies, sports, and the music he made with his brothers. He must have been a bit of a puzzlement to his father—this boy who could mimic anything from ranch hands to the bird calls he studied in the fields outside Annapolis, but who didn't have the inclination to apply himself to his schoolwork. Many years later, in his retirement, the rear admiral taught Sunday school at the First Church of Christian Science in Alexandria. A student in his class describes him as being very warm, but also very strict. "I run a tight ship, Tony," he was told with kind firmness when he came to a class unprepared for the week's lesson.

Mildred Duvall ran a somewhat looser ship those war years, when she was raising her three sons by herself. "It got hard sometimes, because my mother was more lenient and then she'd have to change when Dad got back" is one of the few hints of a filial conflict to which Duvall has ever alluded. He also recalls his father's leaves with much warmth, nostalgically describing squirrel-hunting trips with him.

It would be a mistake to draw any parallels between the Duvall household and that of another military officer, Bull Meechum in *The Great Santini.* If the senior Duvall was disappointed that none of his sons pursued a naval career, if he was somewhat surprised that all three showed such a musical bent, such a theatrical flair, he was also immensely proud of them. The family remained a close-knit and caring one even after all the boys had grown up and moved away from home.

In keeping with their religious convictions, William and Mildred Duvall sent Bodge to Principia Upper School for his high school years. A Christian Science institution in St. Louis, Principia had an excellent reputation as a prep school. The majority of its students were boarders, living on the comfortable and spacious campus, while those whose families were in St. Louis lived at home.

A boarder, Bodge was extremely well-liked because he had such an entertaining personality. His former classmates remember him as fun-loving, thoughtful, and very sociable. While he wasn't an outstanding student, he managed to hold his own at a school with high academic standards. More than his athletic abilities or his musical talents, Bodge's sense of fun is what most impressed people about him in his adolescence. "He always seemed to be part of every activity, and he looked at things and expressed them in a unique way. He was always ready with a funny comment or a funny song," recalls Dawn Larmer, who graduated with Bodge from Principia Upper School in the spring of 1949, and then, like him, went on to Principia College in Elsah, Illinois.

Elsah is a pretty college town, very small and quiet, on the Mississippi River near its junction with the Missouri. Principia is a Christian Science college and does not permit its students to smoke or to drink. In that staid atmosphere, the ebullient Bodge quickly became something of a campus character. "He seemed to be perpetually full of fun," recalls a fellow student.

In his freshman year Bodge wanted to be a typical college student and a really good athlete. "The accomplishments were made in my imagination," he later said of his athletic aspirations. "I was going to be the best in this, the best in that. I participated on a limited and a somewhat ineffectual level because I wasn't mature enough emotionally to even begin to approximate in reality what I accomplished in that same sport in my imagination. . . . I was so afraid of defeat in those early days that I couldn't accomplish anything on any kind of winning level."

While his athletic achievements were trailing his ambitions, Bodge's academic life was floundering. A desultory major in government, he was in danger of flunking out by the end of his sophomore year. His parents were called in for a conference with his professors. With the Korean War raging, it was no time to flunk out of college. An English professor suggested the boy try majoring in drama, and the Duvalls concurred, persuading Bodge to change his major.

"Up to that time I'd looked down on actors," Duvall recalls, "although I used to go to my room and comb my hair like Olivier and recite soliloquies."

Duvall's first drama course was taught by a highly unusual man named Frank Parker, whose background was quite exotic for the Midwest in the early fifties. Trained in philosophy and ballet, he had danced in Pavlova's troupe before the First World War. In the 1920s he was on the Parisian stage performing the *disseur*, a complex one-man repertoire of dance and song. A professor of art history and drama at Principia, he was in his sixties when he taught Duvall. Despite his colorful background, there was nothing bohemian about Frank Parker, who was a serious classicist and thoughtful scholar.

"A universe of such sensibility, his mind was like an extraordinary prism with a vast knowledge of the fine arts, oriental arts, especially Japanese prints, the theater. Going on a train trip with him would be like a semester. His mind was always so alive, so sensitive," says Richard Morse of Frank Parker. Morse, who today has his own mime company in New York, was three years ahead of Duvall at Principia. He was Parker's prize pupil, and when he graduated his mentor turned his attention to Duvall, who then became the primary protégé of this gifted and inspiring teacher.

Richard Morse attributes his appreciation of mime to Parker's influence. A former dancer, Parker was particularly sensitive to movement and taught his students the fine art of graceful gestures. Under Parker's direction, Bodge performed in a full-length mime play, *The Story of Two Pierrots*. He played a traditional harlequin in a production that used Ravel's and Stravinsky's music and was choreographed by Parker.

It was from Frank Parker that Duvall acquired his interest in Arthur Miller's work. For the drama final, Parker had his class perform a play for the whole college. When Duvall was in his course that play was *All My Sons*, and he played the lead, Joe Keller, a ruthless, bombastic middle-aged businessman harboring a terrible secret of greed and betrayal. During one performance, Bodge found himself crying and that clinched it; acting was for him.

"Everyone was talking about Bodge in *All My Sons* because his talent was so obvious," recalls Dawn Larmer, who was as surprised as anyone when the affable, athletic, guitar-playing boy she'd known in high school was turning into an actor overnight. When he played twins in Jean Anouilh's *Ring Around the Moon*, ruffling his hair for the bad twin and smoothing it for the good one, the whole campus was buzzing again about how astonishingly talented Bodge was.

Now his life had the focus it had been lacking, and his parents were very gratified to see the change. They'd taken the advice of the professor who'd urged them to persuade Bodge to change his major; now their flexibility and open-mindedness were rewarded by seeing the transformation in their son from a rather aimless young man to one who was fired with ambition and dedication.

Enraptured with his new purpose in life, Bodge had a strong admiration for the man who'd led him to it. Frank Parker and Bodge Duvall had an unusual trait in common: They each possessed an outrageously playful streak. Once, when the two of them were visiting St. Louis, Parker, walking down the street, suddenly started playing the role of a beggar in a devilishly clever impromptu performance. In a similar vein of nonconformist humor, Bodge turned up at a formal college dance wearing a faded overcoat and made up as a gnarled old man. Hunched over a cane, he wandered among the sedately dancing couples, gazing up at them "with the most extraordinary expression on his face," a classmate recalls.

As he'd been doing since he was four years old, Bodge was using everyone with whom he came into contact as grist for his mimicry mill. Warmly personable and highly sociable, he mingled with everyone, not restricting himself to the small, exclusive clique of drama students. Not only did he enjoy friendships with a variety of different types—he needed to have them. "Then and now he had to have a broad range of friends because he was studying humanity," observes Chuck Hosmer, who now teaches history at Principia.

Hosmer knew the Duvalls from his native Virginia, and he was also in Bodge's class at Principia. The future actor's sense of fun made a strong impression on the future history professor. Hosmer can remember gatherings at the country home the senior Duvalls built on Lake Barcroft, outside of Alexandria, where the three boys would improvise their famous home entertainments and in which Bodge loved to do his own rendition of "The Wreck of Old 99." The country and western songs with which Bodge regaled his audience of friends and neighbors, Hosmer notes, were similar to the ones he would sing as Mac Sledge in *Tender Mercies* thirty years later.

Hosmer's reflections are full of the ebullience that was the Robert Duvall he knew at Principia—the exuberant charmer, the imaginative prankster, the brilliant mimic. Bodge did imitations of a cousin of his from Virginia, a singing evangelist named Fagin Springer, a huge man with a barrel chest who was a real country type. When Hosmer eventually met Springer he was amazed at the accuracy of Bodge's portrayal.

No one, not even his mentor, was safe from that relentless mimicry. In his art history class Frank Parker had each student stand up and give a talk about a painting. When it was Bodge's turn he did a mime of Parker, who had no idea what was going on behind him. The imitation was "gentle but effective," Hosmer recalls with an affectionate chuckle.

He also remembers Bodge at the senior assembly, a weekly gathering in which each senior was given a chance to address his classmates on any topic of his or her choice. For his talk Bodge chose to discuss his family and his life as a Navy brat. Each speaker would sit in an armchair on a platform when addressing the group. Comfortably seated in that chair, Bodge gave a preliminary to his little talk by doing a very clever pantomime of himself stitching his pants.

Another side to Bodge's public life as a senior was his function as Christian Science reader. Every Sunday he'd stand up in the chapel and read aloud alternately from the Bible and the Christian Science manual, *Health and Science*.

Hosmer remembers that Bodge took this role very seriously, although he didn't do much talking about religion.

In college, as it would be throughout his life, Bodge struck all who came into contact with him as being both fun-loving and intense. From the beginning, he was very serious about his acting. He felt deeply in his romantic involvements as well, though on a denominational campus in the 1950s such intensity was likely to restrict itself to the emotional rather than the physical aspects of romance.

But he wasn't the type college women pursued; he was too much of a campus character to come across as good husband material. So it was Bodge who did the pursuing, and once he got a little more help in that area than he would have wanted from his brother Jack, who was as much of a prankster as he was. Their mother sold Christmas cards, and Jack took Bodge's set of cards and mailed them, filled with mushy notes and all signed "Bodge," to girls his brother knew. It wasn't long before replies of the "I never knew you cared," variety started pouring in.

Bodge's years at Principia were full of good times under which the notion to make it as an actor crystallized into a robust ambition. He would have liked to pursue that ambition immediately after college, but the U.S. Army had other ideas. Bodge graduated in June 1953, a month before the end of the Korean War. The draft, though, continued at a wartime rate, and both Bodge Duvall and Chuck Hosmer found themselves in the Army by September of that year at Camp Gordon, near Augusta, Georgia. After the rigors of basic training, Bodge was sent to the Signal Corps school there, where he was trained in radio repair. Hosmer was in the same unit studying sending and receiving, so the two former classmates continued to see each other on a daily basis.

Eager to continue the acting he had started at Principia,

Bodge joined the Augusta Players, an amateur theatrical group that was quickly impressed enough with the young soldier's talents to make him leading man. Military life didn't interfere with Bodge's penchant for mimicry. Quite the opposite. It served to broaden his range because it introduced him to a wider sampling of humanity than he'd met at college.

Bodge and Chuck Hosmer were closer at Camp Gordon than they had been at college or than they would ever be again after their paths in life diverged. Both had girlfriends from Principia who came down together to Georgia for a visit. Hosmer's became his wife but Bodge's girl broke it off, telling him she couldn't marry him because he would never amount to a hill of beans and she'd probably end up having to support both of them for the rest of their lives.

While he was at Camp Gordon, Bodge devoted a good deal of energy to the Augusta Players. One night his barracks was due for an inspection at the same time that there was a Players performance. Determined not to miss the play, Bodge had a friend from another barracks dress up as a civilian and tell the sergeant that he was from the Augusta Players and that they badly needed Private Duvall's participation in their play that night. The imposter's performance was so good that Private Duvall was given permission to skip the inspection so as not to let the Augusta Players down.

Another example of Bodge's playful nature was observed by Hosmer when the two young soldiers took a trip with their mothers to Asheville, North Carolina. Registering at the elegant Biltmore Hotel, Bodge mischievously signed the guest book "Sir Robert Selden, Thane of Lorton," using both his middle name, which is an old Virginia one, and the region of that state from which his father's family came.

Hosmer has many memories of the colorful Private Duvall during their Camp Gordon days, such as the night a bunch of them were in the chapel and Bodge asked if they were familiar with the play *Sleep of Prisoners*. They weren't, so Bodge ran through the whole play for them, playing all the parts himself and getting so carried away with this impromptu one-man show that he poured the contents of the communion pitcher into his army hat.

But Hosmer's fondest memory of his pal from Principia as a soldier is of one night when Bodge was on furnace duty, which entailed stoking the soft coal in the barracks' basement furnaces. The basement window opened a crack and then Bodge appeared in fatigues, totally black with soot, announcing in a sonorous tone, "I am the King of Kings." This was the image that flashed through Hosmer's mind when many years later he saw his old friend portray General Eisenhower on television.

Underlying Bodge's pranks and zest for fun both in college and in the army was the seriousness of his commitment to an acting career. He knew he was good; everyone who saw him act told him so. And he had great faith in Frank Parker's seasoned judgment. Now it was time to find out just how good. The days of college theatricals and amateur performances in Augusta were behind him.

As soon as his army stint was over, Bodge took his GI Bill funds and his hefty ambitions and headed for New York. He never really left behind that provincial America in which he'd been nurtured, though, because he would re-create it again and again in his finest performances. But his immediate goal was the serious study of his chosen profession. With that goal clearly fixed within him, Bodge enrolled at the renowned Neighborhood Playhouse School of the Theatre as a first-year student in the fall of 1955.

2

THE BEST SINCE BRANDO

"There are only two actors in America. One is Brando, who's done his best work, and the other is Robert Duvall," Sanford Meisner told one of his classes a decade after he taught the intense young man who came to his classroom from Principia College and the U.S. Army.

"The Neighborhood Playhouse School of the Theatre," its catalogue reads, "says to the young person who seeks a training in the theatre arts, 'We offer you a stern apprenticeship of two years under teachers, each of whom is an artist in his field and therefore an exacting taskmaster. Come here only if you are willing to work with the intensity necessary to meet the standards which these teachers will hold for you.'"

In Robert Duvall, Sanford Meisner found a student with all the necessary intensity as well as a great wealth of untapped talent. In Sanford Meisner, Robert Duvall found the exacting taskmaster needed to bring his remarkable talent to the surface. As teacher and student, the two were made for each other.

Through Meisner, Duvall touched hands with an older generation that represented one of the finest traditions of American theater. Meisner's world of the theater was embedded in the passion and ferment that was New York's artistic life during the difficult years of the Great Depression. The child of Jewish immigrants, Meisner graduated from

Erasmus Hall, a high school in Brooklyn, and began study-ing piano at the Damrosch Institute. A classmate there in-troduced him to a young composer named Aaron Copland, who in turn introduced him to Harold Clurman, who put him in contact with an aspiring young actor named Lee Strasberg. Strasberg had an acting group at the Chrystie Street Settlement House on the Lower East Side, from which so much energy was churning in the early decades of this century that would have a powerful impact on Amer-ican styles and thinking.

Through Strasberg, Meisner became part of a small group of fervently idealistic actors, writers, and directors who were searching for an art that would speak to the long-ings of depression-ridden America. They banded together and formed the legendary Group Theatre. Included in the ranks of these vastly talented young men and women who were to have so profound an influence on American theater were Stella and Luther Adler, Franchot Tone, Elia Kazan, Lee J. Cobb, and John Garfield.

Throughout the turbulent 1930s Meisner alternated as director and actor for most of the group's offerings, bring-ing such memorable dramas to the stage as Clifford Odets's *Awake and Sing, Golden Boy,* and *Waiting for Lefty.* In the mid-thirties Meisner went to the Neighborhood Playhouse, while Strasberg eventually headed the Actors Studio.

The Actors Studio became known as the home of the Method style of acting, a highly naturalistic technique in which the actor *becomes* the role he is enacting. According to Meisner, though, it was Marlon Brando who first brought the Method to the Actors Studio, rather than learning it there. It was simply Brando's individual acting style, which was then picked up by other students. "Every creative per-son is a Method actor, and the method is his own way of doing," Meisner maintains.

In his long career as director of the Acting Department at the Neighborhood Playhouse, Sanford Meisner taught a host of students who went on to brilliant Hollywood careers. Gregory Peck was a scholarship student of his in the early 1940s. Steve McQueen, Joanne Woodward, Richard Boone, Lee Grant, Eli Wallach, Jon Voight, and Lorne Greene all studied with him. And in that glittering galaxy of stars it was Robert Duvall who Meisner considers the best actor to come along since Brando!

Although many of his most illustrious students made their fame and fortune in movies, Meisner always felt that the stage was a more exalted means of dramatic expression than the far more lucrative screen with its mass audience appeal. "Working on stage is living on a higher level," is the way he put it, claiming that the movies called for a special brand of personality that could handle "the magnifying power of the camera."

Meisner's goals for his drama students were as lofty as his feelings about the theater. He firmly believed that it was the first task of the aspiring actor to sharpen his sense of truth, and he gave over the first months of his classroom work with new students to exercises designed to allow them to develop the ability to react truthfully. Meisner wanted his students to be able "to receive and to respond, to be affected by someone and in turn to affect, and to do these things without forcing or falsifying any response."

It was only after months of training the student in the reality of receptivity and response that Meisner let him get a script in his hands. In this approach he was following closely the lines suggested by the great Russian drama teacher and theoretician Stanislavski. In his three books, *An Actor Prepares, Building a Character,* and *Creating the Role,* Stanislavski laid down the structure for training drama students. All those exercises through which Meisner put his new students were based on the material in *An Actor Prepares.* Strolling through Central Park during the first week of classes at the Neighborhood Playhouse, Jane Feltus saw one of her fellow new students sitting by himself on a bench engrossed in a book. A glance at the title told her that Bobby Duvall was avidly reading *An Actor Prepares.*

He was drinking it all in—the prestigious school, the celebrated teacher, the excitement and energy of the city—with all the exuberance of one who is young, tremendously talented, and infinitely impressionable. That talent was as quickly recognized in the graceful five-story building in Manhattan's discreetly elegant East Fifties that housed the Neighborhood Playhouse as it had been on the campus of Principia College in Elsah, Illinois. "There was no question," said Paul Morrison, who was subsequently director of the Neighborhood Playhouse, "that Duvall had power and talent and dedication. His range was phenomenal."

When his class put on a production of "The Midnight Caller," a work written for the "Philco TV Playhouse," one of the famous drama programs of early television, Duvall was given the leading role of a young man waiting with anguished emotions for his girl to come out of the house. The author of the play came to watch one of the Neighborhood Playhouse performances and was deeply impressed by Duvall's portrayal of his character. The playwright, a highly prolific dramatist from Texas named Horton Foote, would play a pivotal role in Duvall's career.

Bobby had put his usual all into rehearsing "The Midnight Caller." "The only way I can help you with this scene," Meisner told him, "is to say that you must be crying your heart out, and I don't mean allegorically." Bobby came on stage sobbing so uncontrollably that he couldn't speak. "That's it," Meisner said, "but we've got to hear the lines."

Years later Duvall told an interviewer that he had been

able to draw on his own fears of rejection at that time. "When I'd call a girl I'd practically vomit in the phone booth. I don't know if I could do that midnight caller scene today. Success relaxes a man. It's easier for me to meet women."

At the end of the second year, each Neighborhood Playhouse class would do a public production, a kind of showcase. Duvall's class did Tennessee Williams's flamboyant play *Camino Real*. He played the guitar-strumming Byron, a complicated role he interpreted with a great elegance of style. That concluded his course of study at the Neighborhood Playhouse, but he continued to work with Meisner, who privately tutored students, in a professional class.

His years of formal study over, Duvall had to face the harsh, cruel world of a young actor trying to break into the theater. There was a long, lean period in the late 1950s and early 1960s of scrounging around for jobs to sustain him until he got a part, and then in between parts. He had the usual variety of odd jobs that keep creative young spirits going during their first years in New York: working the midnight shift at the post office, washing dishes, moving boxes at the Gertz department store, pushing clothes racks through the garment district, delivering messages at a dollar an hour. One job he simply couldn't hack was washing dishes at Mary Elizabeth's, a prim tearoom and restaurant in Murray Hill. He lasted one day, and then sent Gene Hackman over the next to pick up his paycheck for him.

Hackman understood because he was in the same boat. An ex-Marine, six feet two inches tall and weighing 200 pounds, the rumpled actor back from an apprenticeship at the Pasadena Playhouse shared Duvall's passion for acting— and his poverty. Hackman liked to joke that he got his start on Broadway—as a doorman at a building on Times Square. He was "discovered" there by a former marine officer who walked by, seemingly taking no notice of him but muttering, "Hackman, you're a sorry son of a bitch."

A tough guy who'd been knocking around since his father split when he was thirteen, Gene Hackman had had his share of disasters—like the time in the Far East with the Marine Corps when he drove his motorcycle up the back of a tractor he didn't see at night and severely injured his leg for his carelessness. And the circumstances under which he met his future wife, a secretary named Faye Maltese, were typical of the chaotic quality of his life at that time. They met a dance given by the YMCA, where Hackman had rented a room. But he'd been locked out of it for nonpayment of the rent, so he had no access to his clothes. The first thing Faye noticed about Gene was that he had no socks on.

Doorman, truck driver, shoe salesman, soda jerk: Hackman's jobs were very much on a par with Duvall's. There were nights when Bobby slept on Gene's floor. "It didn't bother me; all I thought about was acting. Not to get on television or anything. Just to do it. I loved it all."

"There's a guy coming to New York you'll really like," Hackman told Duvall one day; "his name's Dusty Hoffman." Hoffman, who had been at the Pasadena Playhouse with Hackman, began his New York life sleeping on his friend's kitchen floor. His roster of jobs is every bit as menial as Gene's and Bobby's: checking coats at the Longacre Theatre, serving as a custodian of a dance studio, demonstrating toys in Macy's.

When an interviewer once asked Duvall if he and Gene Hackman and Dustin Hoffman ever dreamt in those days of youthful struggle that they would become so successful, his reply was: "I always thought I'd do something. I didn't have any specific plan. I didn't know what it was that you had to get to make a mark. I just wanted to keep working, and as it would be revealed to me, then I would do it. I don't know about Gene. He never voiced that. He was humble about it, yet I'm sure that he knew he had the goods and that he had certain things set. He didn't talk about it. Everybody I ever thought was really talented who stuck to it began to make it." But in those early days, as Dustin Hoffman noted later, making it "simply meant working regularly in the theater, going from role to role. . . . Acting is the only art form I'm aware of in which you cannot practice your craft and be unemployed at the same time."

Of course they didn't stay unemployed for long; it only seemed so at the time. There was summer stock, and soon there were TV parts offered from time to time. They formed a loosely connected group held together by the strong bonds of present poverty and future promise—Duvall, Hoffman, Hackman, James Caan, Jon Voight, and a few others. They ran an informal series of poetry readings, they lent one another money and moral support, and they partied. Hackman, who was exactly Duvall's age, was already married, but Hoffman, who was six years their junior, was still single. Bobby was a bit in awe of Dusty's successes with women. "Dustin has had more girls than anyone I've ever known—more even than Joe Namath ever dreamed about."

Duvall clearly remembers Hoffman's technique when the two shared an apartment for a while in 1959. They would be in a coffee shop when the waitress came over to take their order. "How would you like your coffee?" she would ask Hoffman.

"Black, with sugar and a kiss," Hoffman would reply, fixing his devastating eyes on her. And occasionally he would get it, Duvall noted with surprise; even before he got to be well known, Dusty Hoffman had whatever it took to elicit a bit of affection from a harried New York waitress.

Bobby was not exactly inactive in the romance department. He was usually involved with someone or other, at his usual high level of intensity. The grueling task of carving a place for himself in the city's almost impenetrable theater world didn't dampen his customary enthusiasm for having a good time. He and Dustin Hoffman clowned around a lot at parties with an inimitable style, making a great team for acting out dirty jokes. Hoffman did jazz dances to Ray Charles music and Duvall played the guitar with as much gusto as ever.

Everyone who knew Bobby Duvall during that period was impressed with how basically confident he was—not so much of succeeding with a splash, but of getting the opportunity to prove himself as an actor. He had the same faith in Sanford Meisner's judgment that he had had in Frank Parker's, and Meisner had told him that he was the greatest actor to come along since Brando.

Unlike Dustin Hoffman, who, after being told he was "uncastable" enough times, began to think about a career as a director, Duvall never seems to have doubted that he would be able to continue acting. His remark that he just wanted to keep working and, as it would be revealed to him, do it, has an almost religious ring. His faith in himself as an actor may have been connected with the faith he had been taught as a child. You don't expect to become a movie star; you just keeping working at what you feel you must do and the next step will be revealed to you.

His living arrangements in those hungry years were full of the flavor of youthful artistic struggle. He shared an apartment with Richard and Bobby Morse. Richard, who had been Frank Parker's protégé before Duvall at Principia, and his brother were both trying to break into the theater. The other inhabitant of the Hell's Kitchen railroad flat was Vladimir Kostinoff, an émigré from the Soviet Union who was studying choreography. Everyone was broke, and they ate a lot of kasha.

Richard Morse remembers the Duvall of that time as being very direct, very reactive, filled with energy, somewhat rebellious, and volatile. He says his roommate was a very private person who had a strong sense of humor of the country variety. He would call people "hoss" in the western fashion and was given to a lot of clowning around.

There was a mercurial electrical energy to their lives then because things were changing so rapidly. "My roommate was Bobby Morse, and we were starving. Then one day he got the lead in *The Matchmaker*. It happened just like that for him."

It happened for Duvall too—not as dramatically, but he definitely got his first break. He'd been doing summer stock at the Gateway Playhouse in Bellport, Long Island, a theater owned by friends of his, the Pomerans, who had also provided Gene Hackman with work. An intelligent young director named Ulu Grosbard was working there, and he put on a one-night-only studio production of Arthur Miller's *A View from the Bridge* with Duvall playing the leading role of Eddie Carbone.

It must have been quite a sight: the sandy-haired actor with blue eyes whose customary tone was soft and southern playing the beefy, swarthy longshoreman with his Sicilian mannerisms and Brooklyn accent. Even without these differences between the actor and the role, Eddie Carbone is not an easy part to play.

A View from the Bridge is the story of an ordinary man in the grip of an extraordinary passion that he not only does not understand, but also cannot even acknowledge. Eddie Carbone is a vigorous man in the prime of his life, a respected figure in his community of first- and second-generation Sicilian immigrant dock workers. The tension in

Eddie's home life has been growing as his unconscious passion for his niece festers beneath the surface of a solid family life. Catherine, the daughter of Eddie's wife Beatrice's sister, has been raised by the Carbones since her mother died when she was a child. Now a young woman, she is the epitome of virginal loveliness and Eddie is deeply drawn to her, but is unable to face this illicit attraction.

The catalyst for the action of the play is the arrival of Rodolpho and Marco, two illegal immigrants from Sicily whom Eddie takes into his home and for whom he finds work on the docks. Rodolpho, a handsome, amiable young man, and Catherine fall in love. In a frenzy of jealousy he never admits even to himself, Eddie betrays the two men to the immigration authorities. In doing this he is going against one of the most basic rules of the society in which he lives. He's killed in a duel with Marco, but his real destruction happens when he goes against the code in which he has been raised.

Arthur Miller has described Eddie Carbone as a man in the grip of "a passion which despite its counteracting the self-interest of the individual it inhabits, despite every kind of warning, despite even its destruction of the moral beliefs of the individual, proceeds to magnify its power over him until it destroys him."

A challenging role, indeed! And especially so for Duvall, because the illustrious playwright was in the audience. It had been only a few brief years before that Bodge Duvall had played another of Arthur Miller's leading male roles, in his college production of *All My Sons*. In the middle of his portrayal of the ruthless manufacturer harboring a terrible secret, Bodge had found himself crying and had known he'd found his calling in life. Now, playing the blustering, tormented longshoreman in front of the playwright he so strongly admired, Robert Duvall took a big step toward the recognition he needed to find a footing in the theater world.

Like Willy Loman in Miller's acclaimed drama *Death of a Salesman* and Joe Keller in *All My Sons,* Eddie Carbone in *A View from the Bridge* was an ordinary middle-aged man whose fate was given mythic proportions by the playwright. Seeing the young Duvall bring one of his "Everyman" roles to such vivid life must have been as thrilling an experience for Arthur Miller as it was for the rest of the audience, among whom were some prestigious people from New York's theatrical and television industries. Within two months Duvall had a meaty lead in an episode of the TV series "Naked City," playing a gunman on a roof, and his career started moving. It would be a few more years before he could stop worrying about where the rent money was coming from, because the TV work wasn't steady, but it was work and it was excellent exposure.

"Naked City," "The FBI Story," "Armstrong Circle Theater," "Route 66," "Kraft Suspense Theater," "Alfred Hitchcock Presents," "The Twilight Zone," "The Outer Limits"—Duvall did them all, including an NBC Network Spectacular, "John Brown's Raid," with James Mason. A particularly challenging role was another special, "Destiny's Tot," adapted for television by S. Lee Pogostin from *The Fifty-Minute Hour,* a best-selling book about psychoanalyst Robert Lindner's most memorable patients. He had the leading role of a self-aggrandizing, alienated young man with an attraction to the trappings and mentality of fascism. It was a fascinating portrait of how a personality disturbance can take on political overtones, and it showed just how brilliantly Duvall could play an unsympathetic role. He also played in another TV drama written by Pogostin, this time an original script with the fetching title "An Early Morning of a Bartender's Waltz."

As his stage performance of *A View from the Bridge* provided Duvall with TV offers, so his television credits led to more theater offers. He continued to play summer stock at the Gateway Playhouse in Bellport, which had given him his one-shot chance at Eddie Carbone. Then there was one off-Broadway disaster, a very mediocre production at the Gate Theatre of George Bernard Shaw's social satire about bourgeois respectability and the then-taboo subject of prostitution, *Mrs. Warren's Profession.* In it, Duvall was cast as the simpering son Praed, a role the critics admitted was a particularly difficult one. The play opened one night in the summer of 1958 and closed two nights later. Duvall has never gotten over a review in the *New York Post* that said, "Shaw has invented some strange men in his plays, but never one so impossible as the romantic young lead in this," or another review that compared him to Liberace.

By 1961 Duvall had sufficiently proven himself to be offered a leading role in an off-Broadway production. *Call Me By My Rightful Name* was a production typifying the creative vitality transforming the small theaters off the Broadway beaten track into the most exciting drama showplaces in America during the late 1950s and early 1960s. Its producer, Judy Rutherford, only twenty-three, was the secretary to Circle in the Square's José Quintero, whose production of Eugene O'Neill's *The Iceman Cometh* was credited by many as ushering in the off-Broadway theatrical renaissance a few seasons earlier. The playwright, Michael Shurtleff, was young and untried, and the cast was composed of three beginners.

The play is about a trio of maladjusted Columbia University graduate students and it deals with race relations, a theme that was just beginning to make itself felt in the popular consciousness. Duvall played Doug Watkins, a self-styled oddball; his black roommate was played by a young choreographer and dancer named Alvin Ailey, and the curious girl who becomes involved with both of them was portrayed by Joan Hackett. "Robert Duvall accomplishes the difficult task of never letting himself seem to understand his own motives even when the playwright spells them out," observed one critic in the stream of positive reviews heaped on this youthful cast.

The following year Judy Rutherford put on another play, *The Days and Nights of Beebee Fenstermaker,* the longest-running off-Broadway play of the 1962–63 season, in which Duvall was cast as a slow-witted Southerner. It was a part he was to play later in a serious context, but as Beebee's suitor it was a comic one.

Beebee Fenstermaker is a girl who "takes vitamin pills daily and thinks of suicide once a week," reads one of the play's press releases. The play by William Snyder is about zany ambition in New York. In this story of self-deception and self-recognition, Beebee Fenstermaker is a young woman from a provincial town who comes to New York hell-bent on making it as a novelist, or a pianist, or a tap dancer, or a ballerina. She keeps herself ferociously busy and is constantly nagged by the sense of time passing by, mocking all she wants to accomplish. She expects too much of people, and she gives too much. She's possessive and demanding and she drives away the man she loves. In the throes of a desperate loneliness, she seizes on a doltish, good-natured Southern guy who for the moment seems to satisfy her craving for a connection with another human being.

The meaty role of the feisty, frenetic Beebee was played by Rose Gregorio, and the play was directed by Ulu Grosbard, whom she was to marry a few years later. Duvall had already worked with Grosbard on that single but pivotal performance of *A View from the Bridge,* and would work with him again many times in the future. Throughout their long professional and personal association, Grosbard would be the director in whom Duvall had the most confidence. Like himself, Grosbard and Gregorio were fiercely talented and just starting to win the recognition they so much deserved, and Duvall quickly found twin kindred spirits in the intellectual director and the warmhearted actress.

Rose Gregorio had longed to be an actress since she was a small child growing up in a family of Italian immigrants in Chicago. Her parents bound her to a board for the first six months of her life in a traditional preventive measure against rickets. Her father was a plasterer's hod carrier who was determined to give his spirited daughter the education he never had. Gregorio first went to Northwestern University and then on to study at Yale's prestigious drama department. From New Haven she came to New York and went through the usual string of tedious jobs waiting for a break into the theater.

Beebee was her first break, and she did a magnificent job of it, raking in rave reviews for her portrayal of the vibrance and ferocity of Beebee Fenstermaker. Duvall, too, was collecting some critical acclaim for his characterization of the "undemanding simpleton." "Very funny in the play's juiciest role" and "extraordinarily rewarding to watch" were the sweet phrases nestled in the reviews.

As actor and director, Duvall and Grosbard clicked right away. Their backgrounds couldn't have been further apart, but they shared a passion for the theater and an ingrained belief in themselves. Grosbard's childhood had taught him that nothing is to be taken for granted—not even survival. The son of a Jewish diamond merchant, he was born in the Belgian port city of Antwerp in 1929. In 1943 his parents fled the Nazi occupation and began a perilous exodus through France into Spain, managing to squeeze onto a refugee boat bound for Cuba. In his teens, Grosbard spent five years in Havana cutting diamonds and waiting for a visa to the United States. It finally came through in 1948 and he quickly entered the University of Chicago, earning a BA and then an MA in English before going on to graduate study at Yale, where in 1953 he met Rose Gregorio.

Grosbard's first New York job was as a messenger, and he obtained it by knocking on doors listed under "Motion Pictures" in the Yellow Pages. This same persistence got him into a TV movie company in Yonkers, where he scrambled his way up from gofer to production manager. In 1962 Grosbard was assistant director to Elia Kazan on *Splendor in the Grass,* the sensitive portrait of first love starring Natalie Wood and Warren Beatty. Subsequently, he was assistant director on *The Hustler, The Miracle Worker,* and *West Side Story,* and made his off-Broadway debut directing Sean O'Casey's *Bedtime Story.*

With colleagues like Grosbard and Gregorio, with friends like Hackett and Hoffman, with the "juiciest role" in an off-Broadway hit, Duvall's New York life was going wonderfully well. But nothing stands still for long when dreams are being realized. Between *Call Me By My Rightful Name* and *The Days and Nights of Beebee Fenstermaker,* Duvall had already been to Hollywood to make a movie, *To Kill a Mockingbird,* and he was scheduled to make another, *Captain Newman, M.D.* He decided to give Hollywood living a try for a while, saying later that he'd left New York to forget about a woman.

He'd be back before very long, but with a new family, more responsibilities, and new career opportunities. So *Beebee Fenstermaker,* that colorful portrayal of youthful ambition in Manhattan, marked the end of just that phase in Robert Duvall's life. He was still living on the Upper West Side with an assortment of roommates; at that point they were his brother Bud, who was studying opera, and Wayne Vroom, an old friend from Principia. It was the kind of life he loved: lots of laughter and banter and music making, and plenty of girl friends. He'd been dating Scotty McGregor, an actress several years older than he, and he seemed to his friends to be very involved with her. But then his involvements were usually intense; everything he did was intense because he did everything fully and wholeheartedly.

In New York, Duvall had molded his raw native talent into a unique acting style. His student days were over, and now so were those years of artistic apprenticeship and financial struggle. He'd built up a solid reputation with summer stock, TV dramas, and off-Broadway productions. Now another medium was available to him that might lead to a spectacular commercial success, but could break his commitment to artistic integrity.

Just as he'd come to New York with the ideals and discipline instilled in him in his childhood, so Duvall now went to Hollywood with the standards of excellence his drama studies and acting experience had generated in him. He wanted to act in movies and he wanted to continue to develop his burgeoning talent. With his customary sense of purpose and zest for new experience, Robert Duvall was firmly convinced he could do both.

3

THE MOCKINGBIRD
OPENS THE DOOR

To Kill a Mockingbird was as authentically a southern production as a breakfast of biscuits and grits. It was adapted from Harper Lee's 1961 Pulitzer Prize–winning novel of the same name by Horton Foote, who understands that problematic region as much as anyone. A fifth-generation Texan born in the little town of Wharton, where his family ran a store and cotton farm, Foote turned to that setting again and again in the numerous plays he wrote for the theater and for television. He had a deep feeling for the Lee novel and knew how essential it was to find the right actor for the crucial role of Boo Radley. Recalling a performance he had viewed of his TV drama "The Midnight Caller" at the Neighborhood Playhouse, Foote remembered the acting student who had sobbed uncontrollably in the role of the anguished young man. He knew Robert Duvall was right for Boo Radley, and he saw to it that the young television and off-Broadway actor was offered the part.

If ever a role presented a challenge for a screen debut, Boo Radley was it. He's at the heart of the story but isn't on screen until the final scene, where he has to convey worlds of feeling without one word. If ever there was an actor who could meet such a challenge, it was Robert Duvall.

"A day was twenty-four hours long but seemed longer. There was no hurry, for there was nowhere to go, nothing to buy, and no money to buy it with. . . ." Kim Stanley's voice-over reads from the opening pages of *To Kill a Mockingbird* as black-and-white traveling shots reveal the grubby small town in the heart of the Southland as it would have looked on a typical afternoon during the Great Depression.

That soft, Southern-accented voice narrates the story as the grown-up Scout Finch recalls her childhood in an Alabama town. Scout is played by nine-year-old Mary Badham, who had never acted before and was picked for the part at an audition in Birmingham. Somewhere between an urchin and a poet, Scout sees the adult world around her through the perceptions and distortions of childhood. Most of the movie takes place over two summers and is seen through the eyes of Scout, her brother Jem, and their neighbor's houseguest, a chatty little boy, Dill Harris, who Harper Lee had based on her old friend Truman Capote.

Universal had spared nothing to create an authentic atmosphere, scouring the Los Angeles environs until they found a community of clapboard houses with just the right faded look (they were about to be razed by the bulldozer to make way for a freeway extension). The houses were carefully dismantled and then rebuilt on the set.

The cast was as authentic-looking as the architecture. Gregory Peck played Atticus Finch, Scout and Jem's father. In a stiff collar, straw hat, three-piece suit, and steel-rimmed glasses, he looked every inch the modest country lawyer. A widower, Atticus is a gentle man whose love for his children lights up his life. He's also a man with unsuspected depths of courage that are brought to the surface when the court appoints him to defend a black man accused of raping a white woman.

Like the book, the movie meanders along as leisurely as a Southern summer afternoon, loosely interweaving the two threads of the children's fantasy world and the ugly reality of the adult one around them. Boo Radley looms large in the children's fears. He's the grown-up son of the family that lives in the ramshackle house across the street and he's known to be crazy and dangerous, so much so that his father chains him to the bed during the day and lets him out only at night.

Scout, Jem, and Dill make timorous nocturnal forays to the Radleys' front yard and then run in terror from Boo's stalking shadow. An air of mystery clings to Boo Radley, which is enhanced when the children find soap carvings in their likenesses hidden in the hollow of the tree in front of the Radley house.

Meanwhile, they are subjected to disquieting revelations from the adult world as their father prepares his defense of the accused black man. They are spectators in the courtroom when Atticus proves beyond a reasonable doubt his client's innocence. But reason doesn't prevail in the Deep South in the 1930s; Tom Robinson is found guilty. Atticus is already planning an appeal when he hears that Tom has been shot trying to escape from jail.

The narration then jumps from that summer night following the trial to an autumn evening when the children are walking home from an agricultural show, Scout still dressed in her role as a ham. Suddenly, they are attacked by their father's enemy, Bob Ewell, the father of the girl who accused Tom of raping her. Bob's mean-drunk and he attacks the children viciously. Jem's knocked unconscious and Scout manages to struggle out of the costume that's obscuring her vision in time to see a shadowy figure fleeing the scene with the injured Jem in his arms, while Bob Ewell lies dead of a knife wound on the ground in front of her.

Dashing home, Scout is embraced by her father and then led up to the room where Jem is lying in bed. With her father and the sheriff hanging on her every word, Scout relates as much as she knows of what happened to Jem. Then Atticus points to the man standing behind the door and says that he's the one who carried Jem home. The scrawny little girl looks up at the man in the corner and finds herself face to face with the dreaded Boo Radley.

Duvall gives the impression of a height and hulk he in fact lacks as he stands there staring at the wide-eyed child. His pallor is that of someone who is virtually a prisoner; his fair hair looks white, matted. And his face is luminous. It positively glows with the goodness of an infinitely gentle person, a child-man of limited intelligence but of limitless feeling. The recognition that flows between Scout and Boo is one of those magical moments very few movies have ever achieved.

Then Atticus graciously introduces his daughter to Boo, bestowing on the retarded recluse the dignity of his real name, Arthur, and humbly shaking the hand of the man who has saved his children's lives. Atticus and the sheriff neatly find a way to protect the painfully shy Boo from the publicity the news of the rescue would provoke. Scout leads Boo over to say a good-night to the sleeping Jem, who, thanks to him, will be all right.

Scout and Boo sit on the hammock on the Finch front porch together, the small girl and the large man gazing at each other in a rapture of innocent fondness. Then Scout takes her new friend's hand and very gently leads him back to his house.

The Boo Radley role is pivotal to the plot and the atmosphere of the picture. It's in his rescue of Scout and Jem that the two threads of the story come together as the phantom of the children's fantasies saves them from the menace of the real world. Not only must he save them, he must also convey the antithesis of the evil that has almost destroyed them. And he must do it without a word!

The juxtaposition of evil and innocence has been a theme of American Southern literature since *The Adventures of Huckleberry Finn.* It's at the heart of both the book and the movie *To Kill a Mockingbird* as Scout's story reaches its perfectly plotted climax. And it all depended on a bit player who had less than five minutes on camera to present a wordless rendition of the beauty of absolute innocence.

The beatific expression on Duvall's face and the glow suffusing his features as he lights up the conclusion of the picture made quite an impression on moviegoers. It would be years before they connected that luminous face with the other roles in which they were to see the versatile Duvall, and only then because he would become so well-known that his past roles would be recalled in articles and interviews. But anyone who saw *To Kill a Mockingbird* remembers Boo Radley in that final scene.

The movie itself drew a large amount of critical and popular praise. It was timely because the year it was released, 1963, saw Southern racial problems exploding into headlines with sit-ins, freedom rides, and mass demonstrations. And it was also as timeless as childhood dreams and fears.

In fond memory of the role, Duvall has named a succession of his dogs Boo Radley. The film would prove a hard act to follow because movies with that much substance and a part with that type of challenge don't come along often. In the following years Duvall would make many movies that couldn't measure up to *Mockingbird,* playing a wide variety of roles that didn't call for the depth of performance the Boo Radley one demanded. But he would extract from each role, however flimsy, as much as was humanly possible, and he would treat each movie as seriously as if it were another *To Kill a Mockingbird.*

His next part was one of the better ones of Duvall's early movie career. It was in *Captain Newman, M.D.,* a film released by Universal in February 1964. Based on the best-selling novel by humorist Leo Rosten, the movie related the experiences of an Air Force psychiatrist. The lead role was played by Gregory Peck, giving Duvall a chance to see a star in two successive and very different parts.

Captain Newman, M.D., received positive reviews from critics who in those pre-*M*A*S*H* days were taken aback by a film that could be funny about the neuropsychiatric ward of a World War II military base. *The Saturday Review of Literature* said that the film "so deftly blends horror with humor and shock with slapstick that the subject never becomes distastefully crude or depressingly clinical."

The film focuses on three of the patients—played by Bobby Darin, Eddie Albert, and Duvall—the sardonic but compassionate Newman treats. Albert plays a schizophrenic colonel who commits suicide by taking a dive from a water tower, and Duvall plays Captain Paul Winston, reduced to a catatonic state by his guilt over having hidden in a cellar for a year in Nazi-occupied territory. It was a dynamic role because Duvall portrays a man slowly coming out of a severe mental illness and regaining his faculties and personality.

The action takes place in a fictional hospital and was shot on a former U.S. Cavalry outpost in the Arizona desert near the Mexican border. It gave Duvall his first experience with a demanding location and with working with several big-name stars at once, whereas in *To Kill a Mockingbird* he had worked with only one of that caliber, Peck. Now he was cast not only with Peck and Eddie Albert, but also with Tony Curtis, playing Newman's madcap orderly, and with Angie Dickinson, portraying a nurse and providing the psychiatrist with a love interest.

In the movie he made following *Captain Newman, M.D.*, Duvall was cast with the biggest name of all, Marlon Brando, with the venerable E. G. Marshall, and with two rising stars, Jane Fonda and Robert Redford. And the movie was a tremendous flop. *The Chase* is like a Hollywood fable illustrating how a picture can have everything going for it and fall flat on its face. Its failure tells a lot about how movies are made and about how expectations can be dashed by creative, budgetary, or logistical problems. With *The Chase* the problems were essentially of the creative kind because there were conceptual confusions from the beginning that were never clarified.

The film was based on a 1952 Horton Foote play, of which he later wrote a novelization. Like most of Foote's work, its action takes place in a fictional Texas small town. But Foote didn't write the screenplay; for that job producer Sam Spiegel, of *Lawrence of Arabia, The Bridge on the River Kwai, On the Waterfront,* and *The African Queen* fame, chose America's foremost female playwright, the controversial Lillian Hellman. *The Chase* was Hellman's first Hollywood screenplay since she'd been blacklisted in the early 1950s for alleged Communist affiliations.

The director was Arthur Penn, who had directed another Hellman work, *Toys in the Attic,* on Broadway. Penn was one of a school of young New York-trained directors who believed that the cinema could be elevated to an art form through a process of "personal filmmaking" in which the director has the freedom to express his individual point of view.

With a director bent on a personalized touch and a screenwriter needing to prove herself after a fifteen-year exile from Hollywood, it's no wonder that the film ran into difficulties. Their imaginations and creative ambitions were too grandiose. They elaborated on the plot too extensively, overloading it with too much implicit social commentary. As *The New Yorker* astutely put it, "*The Chase* is an opulent melodrama, overproduced by Sam Spiegel, overplotted to the point of incoherence by Lillian Hellman, and overdirected by Arthur Penn."

The skeletal story line is quite literally one of a chase, with Marlon Brando as a conflicted sheriff in pursuit of Robert Redford as Bubber Reeves, an escaped convict and the town's bad boy, but basically a sympathetic figure. The villain is the E. G. Marshall character, the steamy town's powerful and tyrannical millionaire, whose son is having an affair with Bubber's wife, played by Jane Fonda. Hellman envisioned the script as a portrait of an entire society, brashly and sinisterly southwestern, squeezed into the microcosm of a town smoldering with corruption and discontent.

"The whole undertaking is too well-tailored for a community as given to drink, chance, and the horrible accident as this place is, not a surprising result from the creative juxtaposition of Spiegel, Penn, Hellman, Foote, and Brando," wrote Archer Winsten in the *New York Post*.

"A phony, tasteless movie" was the way Bosley Crowther put it in *The New York Times*. One of the scenes the critics found to be in particularly unfortunate taste was the last one (which was not in Horton Foote's script), where the captured Bubber Reeves is killed by a gunman in front of the courthouse, an obvious reference to the gunning down of Lee Harvey Oswald in Dallas a few years earlier—and a totally unnecessary one, it was widely felt.

"A mishmash of Peyton Place sociology, Western mythology, and Deep South psychology," Judith Crist said in the *New York Herald-Tribune*. "Instead of the revelation of situation or character one would expect from those involved, instead of the intellectual challenge and stimulation and fulfillment, we have some very polished professionalism applied to what is, alas, a pretty old Stetson."

Even in a picture as problematic as *The Chase,* with so

many big names to crowd out the lesser ones, Duvall picked up praise from the critics for his portrayal of the meek, sniveling bank employee wallowing in subservience to the town's despot while his sexy wife, played by Janice Rule, is notoriously unfaithful to him. "A few performers manage a suggestion of depth in their roles," Crist goes on to say. "Robert Redford is, at very least, the most nearly sympathetic character on hand as the bad boy; Robert Duvall is notable as the sexpot's weakling husband, a sneaky, cowardly kid who never grew up; and Richard Bradford is very good as the nastiest of the town's nasties."

"I had to fight tooth and nail to get decent actors, brilliant ones like Janice Rule and Bob Duvall who practically steal the film," complained Penn in a diatribe against the studio. Penn's complaints were numerous and expressed in his usual forthright style. "I was used merely to move the actors through each shot like horses," he commented. He was chagrined that the final decisions on editing were not his. "I won't touch anything I can't control to the end. And have fun with. Nothing's worth anything if you don't have fun."

Lillian Hellman was equally infuriated because Horton Foote had been called in as a consultant when it became obvious the script had problems. By the time *The Chase* opened in February 1966, it had cost over five million dollars to make, and those most closely connected with it were already deeply disappointed.

Despite its unfavorable reception, *The Chase* had been an interesting experience for Duvall. He got to play opposite a first-rate actress like Janice Rule and to see two other actresses do their best with stereotypic roles—Angie Dickinson as the sheriff's supersweet wife and Jane Fonda as the convict's brash one. He saw a rising star hold his own next to the great Brando, as Robert Redford beautifully handled the role of the doomed Bubber.

He also saw how tricky it is to make a good movie, how even the best producer, director, screenwriter, and stars can't pull it off if the basic material isn't right. He saw the struggle for autonomy of a talented director and an accomplished writer. He saw how a powerful studio like Columbia can invest what was for that time a fortune in a production that simply couldn't make it and buckled under the weight of its own flaws.

By the time *The Chase* opened, Duvall was having an opening of his own, on Broadway. He had three movies behind him, and they represented three very different kinds of Hollywood ventures. *To Kill a Mockingbird* was the zealously faithful rendition of a serious novel; *Captain Newman, M.D.,* was a successful gamble at approaching a somber subject with madcap humor and an underlying compassion; and *The Chase* was a star-studded failure because the many flaws in the writing and direction imposed a lack of credibility on the performers. What all three had in common was that Duvall received favorable critical attention in each of them. From misunderstood mute to recovering catatonic to groveling coward, he showed the range of his ability and gave a hint at the depth of his talent.

That Hollywood period was not only decisive for Duvall's career, it also wrought enormous changes in his personal life. He didn't really like Hollywood, never felt as comfortable there as he had in New York. There was none of the informal conviviality he'd so loved among the struggling young artists of the Upper West Side. The Hollywood social life was built more around planned parties than informal gatherings, and Duvall was lonely enough to make the rounds in his old Chevy. But he didn't like the girls any more than he did the town. They were pretty enough, no question about that, but he didn't find them bright enough.

Then, at one of those parties, he met a woman who met

all his qualifications. Barbara Benjamin Brent was a striking brunette who had once been one of those girls on the Jackie Gleason TV show who would exuberantly cry "And away we go . . ." at the start of the program. Now separated from her husband, Barbara was busy keeping house for her two little girls. Duvall was instantly drawn to her and found that in the wake of the attraction his old shyness with women was returning. He didn't have the nerve to call her up and ask her for a date, but he couldn't drop the idea of seeing her again, so he got a friend to call her for him.

"Bob Duvall would like to go out with you," the obliging friend told her.

"Me go out with a stupid, narcissistic, boring actor?" was her response.

Hardly a propitious beginning. But she did go out with him, and on their first date it quickly became apparent that he was as far from her stereotype of an arrogant Hollywood male as he could be. Duvall took her to a Chinese restaurant. When he opened his fortune cookie, he read its message, blushed, and wouldn't show it to her. Later, she found out that it had said, "You are about to embark on a new love affair." A *shy* movie actor? The lady was intrigued. They began to see a lot of each other and Duvall found he was enjoying her company immensely. Besides, she was safe— no marriage threat here. There was no way an actor who was just beginning to do well could tie himself down with a wife and two children, right? They were married on New Year's Eve, 1964.

Less than a week later the groom was gone—back to New York to start rehearsals for the off-Broadway revival of *A View from the Bridge* under Ulu Grosbard's direction. The bride followed a few weeks later with kids, dogs, and all her belongings in tow.

It was seven years since Duvall had first played Eddie

Carbone and there had been a lot of changes for everyone involved in that one-night-only performance, including those made in the play itself. Duvall had gained valuable experience in off-Broadway theater and in television and had made a start in the movies; Grosbard had recently directed a Broadway hit; and Arthur Miller had written in another twenty minutes to the script and had added an intermission.

Duvall afterward said that that production of *A View from the Bridge* was one of the best things he'd ever done. Certainly, it had to be one of the most fun-filled because he was surrounded by people he cared about. Not only was Grosbard directing and Jon Voight playing Rodolpho to Susan Anspach's Catherine, but also another old friend from Duvall's New York bachelor days was assisting Grosbard—none other than Dustin Hoffman. Dejected by rejections from producers of himself as an actor, Hoffman was trying to build a director's career. But Grosbard knew better.

"Do you know the person here who could best play Willy Loman?" the discerning Grosbard asked Arthur Miller one day during rehearsals. Interested, the playwright looked around to see whom the director could be referring to because the central character of his best-known play, *Death of a Salesman*, has always been a particularly challenging one. To Miller's amazement, Grosbard pointed to his short, swarthy, unremarkable-looking assistant. It turned out to have been a prophetic choice, because nearly twenty years later Dustin Hoffman *would* play Willy Loman on Broadway.

But that was in the future, and so was *The Graduate*, which soon would catapult Hoffman from obscurity as an off-Broadway assistant director to overnight fame as one of Hollywood's hottest properties. When the Joseph E. Levine production of *A View from the Bridge* opened at the Sheridan

Square Playhouse back in 1965, Dustin Hoffman was behind the stage and Robert Duvall was swaggering across it
as the tormented longshoreman.

In building his characterization of Eddie Carbone, Duvall
drew on a variety of sources, building up a composite character. His interpretation of Eddie was partially based on a
construction worker, a second-generation Sicilian from East
Harlem's small Italian community whom Duvall knew when
he was first in New York. He captured perfectly the man's
accent, voice rhythms, stance, and expressions, giving a
flawless imitation of such phrases as "go fuh cawfee" and
"t'row a hump." To supplement his repertoire of New York
working-class mannerisms, Duvall hung around longshoreman on the Manhattan docks, noticing such significant
details as the fact that a longshoreman wears a belt below
his belly to prevent getting a hernia from heavy lifting, that
his trousers are worn low and have a loose fit, and that he
wears several shirts for warmth.

Duvall's portrayal had these details so well in hand that,
watching his performance, a woman in the audience, the
wife of a longshoreman, whispered to a friend, "That's just
the way my husband comes home from work," as Eddie enters on stage distractedly scratching himself.

The Eddie role was beefed up by Miller's additions to the
original script. The major criticism of Miller's work had always been his tendency to universalize the particular, to
mythologize his characters to the point where he deprives
them of their individuality. In this expanded version, Eddie
Carbone is allowed to emerge more fully as a flesh-and-
blood man tormented by what he can't accept in himself
than as a symbol of man as a plaything in the hands of a
fate over which he has no control.

The play did very well, much better than a more lavish
Broadway production of it had done ten years earlier. The

critics were quick to recognize the authenticity of Duvall's depiction of the turbulence and tragedy that were Eddie Carbone. "Eddie is edgy, temperamental, and under a frightful strain, and Duvall plays him with matching temperament and subtlety," read one review. "Robert Duvall realizes the role of Eddie, the longshoreman whose protective love of his niece turns incestuous, more completely, I think, than any actor who's ever played it," wrote Norman Nadel in *The New York World-Telegram and Sun.* "In the crucial role of the embittered Eddie, Robert Duvall is especially fine in suggesting the attempted sense of fun in a man totally without it," commented Richard Watts in the *New York Post.*

Duvall played Eddie from January to June 1965. He won an Obie Award for the role, but had to leave it because he was scheduled for *The Chase.* It was a part he always loved, calling it his Othello. Of all the roles he was to play, Eddie Carbone came closest to tragedy in the classical sense.

Duvall's personal life at that time was far removed from the dramatic excesses of the one he was portraying on the stage. Bobby and Barbara bought a ninety-year-old Dutch colonial house of fifteen rooms and four fireplaces in Tuxedo Park, a New York suburb on the west bank of the Hudson River—farther out than most, but still conveniently commutable to Broadway.

Plunging into this new phase of his life, Duvall did it with all the intensity and purpose that fired his acting career. Whatever he did was a total commitment. When he was a drama student and then an apprentice actor in New York, he'd lived the single life to its fullest, taking juicy bites out of the Big Apple, relishing the whole life-style, the shabby apartments, the variety of roommates from a Russian choreographer to Dustin Hoffman, the music-filled parties, the madcap humor—and, of course, the women.

With the same zeal, he now threw himself into married

life, taking on the roles of husband and father simultaneously. He took both roles seriously. He and Barbara both wanted a quasi-country life; he'd been raised with rural traditions and she had grown up in a suburb. In Tuxedo Park they found as much country as one can have and still get into the city for nightly performances, plus matinees.

Friends of Duvall's who saw him with Barbara's girls were impressed with how seriously he took the father role. He wasn't playing at being a daddy; he was raising two spirited little girls named Susan and Nancy, and he was determined to do it with the thoroughness with which he embarked on all his endeavors.

Duvall's life took on the patterns of familiar routine. He commuted to work from a suburban home, whether work was a Broadway theater, a movie being shot on location, or in Hollywood. Wherever he worked, home was the sprawling house in Tuxedo Park with Barbara, Susan, and Nancy. It was a solid, comfortable life, just the kind he wanted— not exotic or glamorous, but rooted in the traditional family values with which he was raised. As when he'd discovered acting Bodge Duvall found himself in terms of his life's work, so with marriage and instant fatherhood he found a new emotional security.

Concentrating his energies on his career and his new family took almost all his time; what was left over, Duvall devoted to sports. Now that he had a more mature perspective, Duvall was able to focus his attention on one sport at which he was capable of excelling. Tennis was his game, and he attacked it with as much enthusiasm as if his life's goal was to be a pro. When his elitist neighbors balked at having an actor in their exclusive tennis club, the undaunted Duvall simply built his own court. Eventually, he played the club's best members—and won.

The suburban husband, householder, and doting father

was about as far as one could get from some of the parts
Duvall was playing. He turned out to have quite a flair for
villainous roles. Scoundrels are the stuff of melodramas,
and Duvall's first Broadway lead was in a play that, although
it was billed as a suspense thriller, definitely had melo-
dramatic overtones.

Wait Until Dark opened at the Ethel Barrymore Theatre in
February 1966 and starred Lee Remick as the quintessential
heroine. She played a warm, intelligent, courageous, and
lovely young woman who happens to be totally blind. She
lives in a Greenwich Village apartment with her photographer husband, who pushes her to be as independent as possible.

The plot centers around a heroin-stuffed doll a gang of
criminals believes is in her apartment. The opening night
audience was expecting first-rate theater from a star like
Remick and a play written by Frederick Knott, author of the
acclaimed thriller *Dial M for Murder,* the smash hit of a few
seasons earlier. But *Wait Until Dark* was not of the same caliber as the earlier play, as the critics were quick to point out.
The plot was lacking in true suspense; it was contrived and
implausible. Although disappointed in the play, that opening night audience was impressed with the competence of
Lee Remick's performance and with ten-year-old Julie Her-
rod, playing a little girl who is beguiling and sinister by
turn. But it was Robert Duvall who stole the show. Harry
Roat, Jr., the chief of the trio of criminals, is about as bad as
they come—a cold-blooded, sadistic killer who'll stop at
nothing to get what he wants. He played the bad guy so
convincingly that the audience actually booed him during
the curtain calls.

"One of the most villainous villains ever," praised Stewart
Klein, WNEW's theater reviewer. "A lodestone of fear . . .
the ultimate adversary," said Norman Nadel of *The New York*

World-Telegram and Sun. Praises were pouring in for this first Broadway role of Duvall's, but the fact that it was on rather than off that famous thoroughfare didn't make all that much difference to him.

"I prefer a small theater. If I find a good play, I'd rather do it in a workshop than on Broadway," Duvall maintained. Nor was he attracted by the much sought-after long run. "Three weeks at a time—that's the way I'd like to do plays."

But even if he could take his first Broadway lead in his customary stride, *Wait Until Dark* did a lot for Duvall because it showed how versatile he was—from a subservient bank employee in his last movie, to an anguished longshoreman in his last play, and now to a chillingly evil criminal. The breadth of Duvall's range was quickly becoming apparent.

The *Wait Until Dark* script called for him to have a shaven head and to keep changing disguises—wigs, walking sticks, eyeglasses, etc. Why this should be necessary when the woman he was terrorizing was blind is never fully explained, although Duvall did proffer the suggestion that it could be to keep the little girl from identifying him. Weak as the play itself might have been, Duvall's part was a rich one in the sheer flamboyance of the evil of the man. He got a chance to show with a flourish just how vividly he could portray someone without one redeeming human feature. It also showed how well he could handle a multiplicity of disguises.

He was to play the bad guy many more times in numerous movies, and he was to get so proficient at disguise that for a long time the public didn't recognize his own face. A good villain is hard to find and Hollywood's always in need of one, so once again Duvall turned from stage to screen. This time there was no relocation to Tinseltown, because he was firmly settled in Tuxedo Park with his wife and daughters. Hollywood was a nice place to work, but he wouldn't want to live there—and didn't. But work there he did, making movie after movie in which, despite the mediocrity of so many of them, his performances were always gems of extraordinary acting.

He would assume an astonishing myriad of identities in the following years. But at the core of all those elaborate disguises and the vast array of parts was the man himself, doing the best he could to be the best actor he could be. And his best would turn out to be suffused with a genius of which few people were aware back in those days when the mockingbird opened the door on Duvall's movie career.

4

HANGING
AROUND A GUY'S MEMORIES

How does he do it? Duvall is asked again and again how he manages to get a character down to such a perfection of detail.

"I hang around a guy's memories," is his answer. "I store up bits and pieces about him and then use it in the role . . . I especially like to find one or two subtle contradictions in a guy, in order to make him as colorful as possible."

As he did with the Eddie Carbone part in *A View from the Bridge,* Duvall tackled all his movie roles by developing a characterization through his brand of "behavorial research." He would borrow traits from various people in order to build up a composite.

"A script is just words on a page," explains Duvall. "There's an expression like 'a pound of behavior is worth a ton of ideas,' or something like that. An actor takes those ideas and lifts them off a page and transforms them into behavior. My life is geared toward behavior. I need to make something happen at that moment."

Beside being intuitive, Duvall's style is highly individualistic. He has said that an actor lives through his fantasies, that he is paid the salary of his daydreams: "That's all it is—organized daydreams."

This individualistic, intuitive way of working was not to every director's taste, as Duvall explained to Norma McLain Stoop in an interview for *After Dark* in 1973:

"The movie industry is very caste-conscious. It's a director's medium in a lot of ways, and I don't try to be a hard
guy to work with. But I decide what I'm going to do with a
character. I will take direction, but only if it kind of supple-
ments what I want to do. If I have instincts I feel are right, I
don't want anybody to tamper with them. I don't like tam-
perers and I don't like hoverers."

This free-wheeling attitude was bound to clash with particularly authoritarian directors like Henry Hathaway, who
directed *True Grit,* in which Duvall played the outlaw chief
who rides into John Wayne's ambush. Hathaway had a reputation for making grown men feel like little boys, a directorial style that Duvall couldn't abide.

Duvall refused to take the director's word as law on the
set. When Hathaway told Glen Campbell, who was playing a
Texas Ranger, to tense up at a certain moment, Duvall took
exception to this because in his opinion it was a point where
Campbell should be relaxing. "It's like telling a trapeze artist to fall" was the way he later explained it.

The next day Hathaway gave Duvall a direction he didn't
like, and the actor blew up. Hathaway shouted back and
Duvall, his eyes an icy blue in a face of granite, threatened
to bring up Hathaway in front of the union, using some
four-letter words to drive his point home. When Hathaway
criticized his language, Duvall roared back, "Why not—*you*
use it."

"I do believe Henry's got the boy's dander up," was John
Wayne's comment as "The Duke" watched with amusement
the heated encounter between the imperious director and
the rebellious actor. That fiery exchange, however, cleared
the air and they all settled down to make the movie that
won Wayne an Academy Award.

While there was no doubt that Duvall had his difficulties
with directors, there was one besides Ulu Grosbard whom

he deeply admired—Francis Coppola. Duvall and Coppola had much in common: They were both in their thirties when they first worked together, although Duvall was the elder by eight years; they were both maverick types wary of Hollywood posturings and politics; and they both clung fiercely to the autonomy of their creative expression.

Coppola was one of the "movie brats," as they were affectionately and exasperatedly known in the motion picture industry. They were a "new breed of young energetic film-school types who were itching to lead the movies into a new age of high-tech, high-art, and high profits," as critic David Sterritt succinctly put it in an article in *The Christian Science Monitor*. Coppola and the other "brats"—Steven Spielberg, Martin Scorsese, George Lucas, John Milius, John Landis, and Michael Cimino—all, according to Sterritt, experienced the "difficulty of joining personal expression with big money and flashy show biz traditions."

Of all his breed, Coppola was the most flamboyant, the most audacious. He made the most money, but then he also went broke just as often. Unlike Duvall, Coppola's background was steeped in theatrical influences. He grew up in Queens, the son of Carmine and Italia Coppola. His father was a flutist, composer, and conductor; his mother was an actress who had appeared in several Vittorio De Sica films. At the age of nine, Coppola was bedridden with polio for a year and developed an interest in comic books, puppetry, and ventriloquism. He was trained for a musical career and was well on his way to being an accomplished tuba player when he switched to drama. He studied theater arts at Hofstra University and then went on to UCLA in 1959, where he did graduate work in film studies.

His first screenplay was an adaptation of Carson McCullers's novel *Reflections in a Golden Eye* as a vehicle for Marlon Brando. The studio, Warner Brothers–Seven Arts, liked his work enough to give him more writing assign-ments. He worked on fifteen scripts, two of which were pro-duced: *This Property Is Condemned* and *Is Paris Burning?* Itching to get a free hand with a film, Coppola jumped at the chance to write and direct *The Rain People,* which was based on a short story he had written in college. Released by Warner Brothers–Seven Arts in 1969, *The Rain People* won the San Sebastian Film Festival Grand Prize in 1970. A quirky little movie, it didn't do well at the box office and received a mixed bag of reviews, some critics finding its pa-thos moving, while others thought its theme sophomoric and its characters' motivations implausible.

Whatever its critical reception, it was a fascinating movie to work on because of Coppola's unorthodox production style. He cast Duvall as a Nebraska motorcycle cop, macho on the outside, hurting and vulnerable within. Duvall's old pal from the hungry years, James Caan, was playing "Killer," a former college football star who is suffering from brain damage caused by a head injury he sustained on the field.

Hitchhiking, Killer is picked up by Natalie Ravenna, played by Shirley Knight, a woman who has just left her suburban Long Island home to drive across the country to think her life over. She calls her husband from the road to tell him that she's okay, but she has to have some time by herself because she's not sure about what she wants and has to absorb the fact that she's pregnant.

From a current perspective, the story line may sound foggy and contrived, but this was in the late sixties, the dawn of the counterculture, the era of *Easy Rider.* Taking off on a cross-country voyage of self-discovery was a reflec-tion of the spirit of restlessness and experimentation per-meating the the culture. For a housewife to make such a journey prefigured the women's liberation movement that was to dominate the following decade.

The unlikely companions, Killer and Natalie, make their way across America, encountering all sorts of bizarre situations. Natalie remains full of questions and eager for experience, while Killer is anything but what his nickname suggests because the brain damage has left him gentle and passive. He clings to Natalie, who can't quite shake him and isn't sure she wants to. They have long, cozy talks. Killer tells her about the rain people, who are made of rain and disappear altogether when they cry, and she feels a kinship with these watery visions who have no substance.

Their journey ends tragically in a Nebraska trailer camp where Natalie is with the macho cop who gave her a traffic ticket earlier in the day. A widower, Gordon lives in a trailer with his teenaged daughter, Rosalie, whose knowing air is disquieting in a young girl. Rosalie and Killer have been wandering around the trailer camp, spying through the trailers' windows at the people within.

Meanwhile, Natalie learns more about Gordon. Behind his tough front is a gentle, suffering man who is still mourning the death of his wife and baby son in a fire. The humanity of the interaction between the runaway wife and the complex cop clouds over when he starts to make love to her and she resists him. They're struggling with each other at just the moment Killer and Rosalie look in on them through the window. Killer rushes into the trailer and starts pummeling Gordon. Rosalie grabs hold of her father's gun and shoots Killer, fatally wounding him.

An offbeat movie, *The Rain People* was shot in a highly original manner. Coppola got a caravan going—eight vehicles moving through eighteen states in as many weeks—all the way from New York to Denver. Coppola's caravan eliminated studio sound stages, sets, offices, and all the usual paraphernalia of movie-making. It was a self-contained mobile motion-picture unit, transporting cast, crew, and equipment, serving as cutting room, wardrobe department, and prop shop.

True to his ideal of cinema verité, Coppola kept the script flexible so that he could incorporate local people and incidents into it whenever it seemed appropriate. This novel approach to making a film fired Duvall's imagination, stirring to life the directorial impulses within the innovative actor. The vast Nebraska plains pulled at all that was country in him. When he and James Caan met the B. A. Petersons, a rugged clan of ranchers and rodeo hands, Duvall was drawn to these rough types who called Caan "Hollywood."

"Being a Jewish boy from New York City, Jimmy naturally wanted to be a cowboy," Duvall told Bart Mills of the *Manchester Guardian*. Duvall, who had spent boyhood summers on his uncle's Montana ranch, wasn't particularly eager to rope steer in ninety-degree heat, but Caan eagerly volunteered for the honor, plunging right in with his customary gusto. "We don't need those ones, Hollywood, they already been branded," the Petersons told him.

Duvall saw a movie in the Petersons, a freewheeling-style documentary about the lives of these resilient rodeo nomads. Recording the Petersons' colorful life-style on film would engage Duvall's imagination, occupy his energies, and drain his checkbook for the next seven years.

We're Not the Jet Set—the film's title delineating the remoteness of its subject from the world of fashion and influence—eventually turned Duvall into a producer as well as a director. He started his own production company, bestowing on it a name right out of western lore—"Che-ku-ee," an Indian call his Montana aunt always used because of its far-reaching range.

Never one to do anything by half measures, Duvall soon involved Barbara and the girls in his directorial endeavor. They would all fly out to western Nebraska when his sched-

ule gave him a free weekend. Working without a script, shooting with 16mm film, improvising all the way, Duvall let the style of the lives he was documenting determine the shape of the film.

They fascinated him. Something in their blatant macho postures filled him with a kind of awe that made him determined to capture it on film. In an *After Dark* interview in 1973, when he was most deeply engrossed in the project, Duvall talked about his perceptions of the Petersons:

> *They're strange people, cowboys. Even the little boys have broke their bones. You know, the one in the N.F.L. who stands out most daring of all is Walt Garrison, of the Dallas Cowboys, and he's a bulldogger in the rodeo in the off-season. They're crazy. No pain. It's somethin' to do with the male image. The whole sense of woman. . . . Some of these cowboys, they feel they're not worthy of . . . I guess they're always seeking. They're rough guys—knockin' each other's heads in and the next day they're good friends. And this family. . . . Like, one boy had broke a shoulder ridin' a steer, cussed the steer, didn't want to go to a doctor. He was about eighty pounds and he and his brother were fightin' like animals and the old man was watchin' it, just lovin' it, and he said, "Wait a minute! You got a broken shoulder. No rasslin'," he says, "only fist fights." It's a different concept of violence. They live closer to it.*

While Duvall was using his spare time to document a contemporary western life-style, he was also working on a movie that was creating a controversial depiction of the historical West. Duvall was cast as Jesse James in *The Great Northfield Minnesota Raid*, a complex film that looked at old legends through modern eyes.

"The outlaws in this movie are born of history but made of myth," wrote Jay Cocks in *Time* magazine of the 1972 version of the notorious bank-robbers-turned-folk-heroes.

Written and directed by Philip Kaufman, the film starts off as straight history but quickly takes on a unique tone of its own. Set in the Missouri of 1876, it opens when state officials are about to grant amnesty to Cole Younger and Jesse James, until a representative of the railroad bribes them into sending a Pinkerton detective to track down the outlaws. Jesse James, who wants nothing to do with any amnesty, has already ridden off with his brother Frank toward Northfield, Minnesota, home of "the biggest bank west of the Mississippi."

Cole Younger, played by Cliff Robertson, had been hoping for the amnesty, but when it's off, he rides after Jesse to join in the raid despite the warnings of a gypsy witch in a scene suggestive of *Macbeth*. Robertson's Cole Younger is a reasonable robber and rational murderer, while Duvall's Jesse James is "a phony populist psychotic with a severe problem of sexual repression," as Vincent Canby perceived him in his *New York Times* review of the film.

"Robert Duvall does Jesse as a psychotic laboring under two delusions: that he is a mystic visionary and that the cockamamie plan to stick up a bank in far-off Minnesota is a guerrilla raid even though the Civil War is ten years bygone," said Richard Schickel in *Life*.

Understanding how Duvall put the Jesse James role together explains a lot about his characterization techniques. He did some historical research and discovered the interesting fact that Jesse's father had been a Baptist minister, so he decided to play the bank robber with a bit of the preacher in him.

Next came the "behavorial research," in which Duvall went to churches around the San Fernando Valley, picking up on various traits of the preachers he saw there. With his usual thoroughness of scrutiny, he noticed the way they inhaled air, almost getting high on it. He used that in his Jesse

portrayal, and he insisted on a bowl haircut that was in style in Jesse's time. In the cave before the raid, Duvall's Jesse "did a little Pentecostal thing."

Delving deeper into the historical Jesse James, Duvall read a book of Pinkerton files because detectives from that infamous agency had been pursuing Jesse James for years and had acquired a wealth of information on the flamboyant bank robber. When he was seventeen, during the Civil War, Jesse dressed up like a woman to spy on Yankee soldiers in a whorehouse. Digesting this information, Duvall chose to play Jesse with a hostility toward women. In fact, he played Jesse James "a little like he could be a little queer." Recalling the crotch orientation of the Peterson clan, Duvall suddenly grabbed another actor by the crotch in one of his Jesse scenes.

"I tried to keep a feeling for the overall myth, the Robin Hood side . . . which wasn't true . . . he didn't give to the poor, he kept it . . . and the folk-hero side. When he died, the headlines in the paper read, 'Good-bye, Jesse.' I loved that."

A scoop of history, a pinch of myth, a sprinkling of psychological interpretation, a mixture of previously observed traits and quirks, and, presto, Robert Duvall has created a character who's a composite of assorted types. He stirs in his own inimitable style a Jesse James who's different from any other portrayal of the legend on the screen; a complete, complex, and, however crazy, comprehensible human being in whose memories Robert Duvall has been hanging around.

The entire production lent itself to zany interpretations, audacious experiments, and risk-taking. "A curious Western, part period pastiche, part slapstick, part bang-bang action, part factual," was the way *Cinema TV Today* categorized the film. Vincent Canby said in *The New York Times* that "by turns the movie is quirky, kinky, goofy, a little Peckinpah here, a little Fellini there, a few references to Vietnam, a touch of gallows humor, and the rather fashionable suggestion that Americans are now and have always been crazy, crooked, and homicidal."

"Director Philip Kaufman serves up an eccentric, erratic mixture of subdued imagery, flamboyant dialogue and down-home movie corn" was the way Jay Cocks saw it. "Starts with an historical approach but winds up as just another killers-and-psychotics-at-play exercise in incredibility," criticized Judith Crist in *New York* magazine.

"A beautiful and simple film about goodness and hope," Penelope Gilliatt said in *The New Yorker*. Gilliatt was very taken with the dynamism of the film's depiction of an historical period, finding it infused with a "contagious sense of amazement that characterizes frontier life and expansion everywhere."

Playing Jesse James called for a high-profile virtuoso performance; playing *THX 1138* called for a very restrained and subdued one. It's ironic that an actor capable of such complex characterizations as Robert Duvall should have for his first movie lead a character who has no name, merely initials and a number.

THX 1138 is the title role in a futuristic fantasy-nightmare. It was the first film produced by Francis Coppola's studio, American Zoetrope, a San Francisco-based outfit the director founded to give creative young talent a vehicle for expression. The movie's writer-director was the twenty-five-year-old George Lucas. Based on a short film for which he won a prize in the National Student Film Festival, *THX 1138* borrows heavily from Orwell and Huxley and experiments freely with hi-tech devices.

The action takes place in the twenty-fifth century in a subterranean city ruled by a tyranny of computers. The story line is a familiar one borrowed from tales of utopias gone haywire. A man and a woman fall in love in a society where that very emotion is a crime. Added to this offense, they commit that of drug evasion to escape the substance fed to the populace to subdue it.

But it is not, as Vincent Canby points out, "as either drama or social commentary that *THX 1138* is most interesting. Rather it's as a stunning montage of light, color, and sound effects that create their own emotional impact. *THX 1138* is practically an iconography of contemporary graphics in which actors are, intentionally, almost but not quite indistinguishable from the decor."

And that's just what Duvall accomplishes—he makes himself virtually invisible. Dressed in a white suit, head shaven, he, like all the characters, blends into the scenery almost to the point of oblivion. He succeeds so well that most of the reviews scarcely mention the acting, but concentrate instead on the special effects.

"Stunning visuals, blinding white corridors and rooms, flickering television sets, filtered voices, and a barrage of electronic bleeps and gurgles surround these pitiful zombies," noted Arthur Knight in *The Saturday Review*.

It was Roger Greenspun in *The New York Times* who observed just how carefully the cast managed to minimize itself, crediting Duvall and Maggie McOmie, who plays his love, LUH 3417, with "lovely performances" suggesting "human identification without highly individualized characterization."

From a legendary bank robber of the Old West to a robotized denizen of a future era, Duvall gave each part exactly what it required. From a highly individualized, intensely dramatic performance to a subtly muted one, he tailored his acting style to the demands of the particular movie he was making.

And there were a lot of them. He played all kinds of cops, from Nestor, who had a penchant for busting gays in *The Detective* (1968), starring Frank Sinatra, to a tough federal inspector partial to both costars, Jennifer O'Neill and Donald Sutherland, in *Lady Ice* (1973), a jewel-heist flop of which *Variety* said: "If the film comes off at all it is due to the superior work done by Robert Duvall, who is rapidly becoming one of the best character actors in the business."

The critics kept noticing how Duvall's ability gave luster to even the most mediocre movies. When he played a ruthless land baron in *Joe Kidd* (1972), starring Clint Eastwood, Judith Crist commented in *New York* that, "Beyond Eastwood, the only notable performer is Robert Duvall, who does his usual excellent job, even as an incredibly rotten, rotten guy."

He received similar notices as a bad guy captured by frontier marshal Burt Lancaster in *Lawman* (1971), a role one reviewer credited with adding "depth and dignity" to the paltry script.

Besides sharing screen credits with glittering names like Sinatra, Wayne, Eastwood, and Lancaster, as well as Steve McQueen in *Bullitt* (1968) and Charles Bronson in the adventure story *Breakout* in 1975, Duvall was frequently featured in pictures in which his old pals had graduated to top billing. He was the grounded astronaut while James Caan was the one who got to go to the moon in the trite spaceflight story *Countdown* (1968), but they both got plenty of action in *The Killer Elite* (1976) as CIA-employed gunmen. In a different vein, Duvall was the old-style Communist in *The Revolutionary,* a 1970 movie starring Jon Voight as a new-style radical. Duvall had a small part as a nameless businessman in Coppola's grim portrait of a surveillance wizard in *The Conversation,* starring Gene Hackman, which was released in 1974—the same year the Watergate disclosures made bugging devices a matter of national interest.

Those two old friends from less prosperous days, Duvall and Hackman, had the interesting experience of playing essentially the same role in two different films. Hackman, who'd come a long way since his doorman days, won an Academy Award for Best Actor of 1971 for his portrayal of detective Popeye Doyle in the fast-paced story of New York drug busts, *The French Connection*. Doyle was based on the spectacular career of a real-life New York cop, Eddie Egan, who totaled a record number of arrests—8,700—in his nineteen-year career with the NYPD. *Badge 373* was to be a semisequel to that tremendously successful film, and initially the central character was to be called Popeye Doyle again. But when Duvall got the part he insisted that the character's name be changed because he didn't want his interpretation of Egan to be inhibited by the public's anticipation of seeing a repeat of Hackman's performance. So it was as Eddie Ryan that Duvall played the role.

But whatever the name, it was still the same tough New York cop. *Badge 373* was as authentically a New York production as *To Kill a Mockingbird* was a southern one. It was shot all over the city in the fall of 1972, with the production units working out of trailers on the Hudson River pier. The screenplay was written by columnist Pete Hamill, renowned for his knowledge of the city's streets and citizens. Many of the small parts were played by off-duty detectives, several of whom were friends of Egan's.

Duvall hung out with these men to prepare for his role, observing with his usual astute eye and ear their mannerisms, slang, and accents. He noted that those who didn't wear jackets, as Egan hadn't, wore their guns under their pants cuffs, and that's where he wore his as Ryan. He gained twelve pounds to give a suggestion of a tough guy going to pot.

Duvall's Eddie Ryan has been suspended from the police force following one of his unorthodox drug raids. Bereft of his badge, 373, he still manages to carry out a private war against his partner's murderers. He's a man who's had everything he's earned in life stripped from him, but who goes after his prey with a stubborn resolve to avenge wrong.

Newsweek's Joseph Morgenstern said that Duvall "out Egans Egan . . . with an accent that wallows in wry New Yorkese, his gestures flit nervously from tenderness to rage; his entire manner conjures up the aging cop who has to fight to get to do his job."

A "two-leveled performance" was how David Sterritt in *The Christian Science Monitor* referred to Duvall's Egan: "A portrayal which becomes doubly convincing as each level increases in depth and complexity. On the surface, Ryan is an out-and-out slob, foul-mouthed, chain-smoking, hard-drinking, womanizing. Yet he believes implicitly in his own sense of honor and in the rightness of his personal crusade."

It was as though Duvall were playing his own version of cops and robbers, switching roles from picture to picture. Right after playing the unsavory but incorruptible Egan, he won the lead in a movie about a man who's just gotten out of prison after doing time for robbing a bank. Only it was a mob-owned bank he and his brother had unknowingly robbed, in retaliation for which the gangsters have killed his brother. *The Outfit* is the story of this ex-con's vendetta against the syndicate.

Playing the cop and the outlaw back-to-back this way was a challenge Duvall relished. Realizing that the two characters shared so similiar an objective as avenging a murder and that they were both lonely outcasts, he still found ways to differentiate between them. He played Eddie Ryan in full-blown bellicose New Yorkese, and the protagonist of *The Outfit* with a Midwestern reserve and self-containment. That ability to perceive the differences in the underlying similarities, and then to differentiate on a more fundamental level, comes from Duvall's sensitivity to individual nuances. He realizes that the villain doesn't see himself as a villain, and his villains are never stereotypes, but expressions of what is unique to each character. Duvall doesn't make his villains sympathetic because he's not a sentimentalist, but he always succeeds in making them plausible, comprehensible people who are internally consistent and who are justifiable to themselves.

Two of Duvall's most memorably unsympathetic roles were in *M*A*S*H* and *Network*. In both these movies, he plays men with unattractive personalities and values. Each of these evokes the audience's contempt, but both are perfect realizations of complete characters.

M*A*S*H was one of those well-coordinated productions where everything meshed. Adapted by the renowned screenwriter Ring Lardner, Jr., from a novel written by Richard Hooker, a combat surgeon, and directed by the brilliant, erratic, and controversial Robert Altman, it starred Donald Sutherland as Hawkeye and Elliott Gould as Trapper John.

The movie takes place in a mobile army surgical hospital in the midst of the Korean War. Doctors and nurses in fatigues dash through the mud to the bloody operating room set up in a tent while the PA blares absurdly incongruous announcements and American songs sung in oriental accents. Altman captures this maniacal atmosphere of the time and place, teeming with chaotic energy and tinged with despair and hilarity.

Hawkeye and Trapper John are the perfect heroes for America at the start of the seventies: Outrageously iconoclastic, they speak for rational and humanist values amid the casual carnage and unfeeling bureaucracy surrounding them. Major Frank Burns epitomizes everything Hawkeye and Trapper despise: incompetence, hypocrisy, and self-righteousness. It was a role that in hands less skillful than Robert Duvall's could easily have slid into crude caricature. But he's so totally the part that Frank Burns comes across more quietly contemptible than flagrantly obnoxious. Burns is a man convinced about his beliefs and his behavior, and Duvall conveys that smug intractability through his every mannerism, facial expression, and tone of voice.

In his *Newsweek* review, Joseph Morgenstern pointed out the pivotal role Duvall's character had in the film's structure: "Sutherland and Gould play brilliantly together in a sly, easy camaraderie of men who love life too much to live by infantile rules. Equally brilliant is a complimentary duet for fanatics played by Robert Duvall and Sally Kellerman. He's a surgeon and religious nut, she's a chief nurse and army nut, and their seduction scene is as funny a bit of business as anything in the movie."

Kellerman got more praise for her portrayal of Major "Hot Lips" Houlihan than Duvall received for his role as her on-screen lover and fellow conspirator against the Hawkeye–Trapper John faction. Kellerman had the easier time of it because her part called for satire with a slapstick tone; she could ham up Houlihan, while Duvall chose to play Frank Burns straight. Hot Lips is riotously funny with her exaggerated expressions and gestures, while Frank Burns is funniest as a foil for Hawkeye and Trapper John.

Duvall's handling of the Major Burns role shows the extent of his restraint. To make Frank Burns flamboyantly odious would be to steal theatrical thunder from the colorful Hawkeye and Trapper John, so he plays him with an admirable understatement. Obscurely obnoxious, Frank's the ideal foil for the good guys, and Duvall keeps him exactly that.

The same restraint can be seen in *Network*, in which Duvall plays Frank Hackett, "a perfectly amoral corporate creep," as Frank Rich described the role in his *New York Post* review. *Network* was the movie in which Hollywood cast a cold and critical eye on its robust rival—television. The plot centers around a network's exploitation of a newscaster's breakdown. Forced off the air because of his program's poor ratings, Howard Beale, played by Peter Finch, threatens on the air to kill himself before the camera in his final appearance.

A wildly ambitious program director, Diana Christensen, cleverly portrayed by Faye Dunaway, seizes on the fact that Beale's outburst has driven his ratings up and gives him a show of his own in which to spout his revulsion at a dehumanized society. In the end, though, Beale's ratings fall to the point where everyone wants to get rid of him, but can't, because the network's eccentric president wants to keep his show going at any cost. Diana, Frank Hackett, and a handful of their colleagues decide that the only way out of their dilemma of low ratings and their superior's wishes is to kill Howard Beale. They arrange to have him shot on live TV, getting rid of his show and its poor ratings and boosting the ratings of their own series about a radical terrorist group at the same time.

Network was contemporary black comedy with some traditional stock characters. There was William Holden as the heroic Max Schumacher, the head of the network's news department, possessed of a sad, defeatist integrity. There was a knight-errant in the form of hapless Howard Beale. Then, for the forces of evil, there was Faye Dunaway as a witchlike opportunist enticing the hero into an improbable affair; and, finally, Robert Duvall as a prosaic kind of villain.

Again, Duvall plays the villain with a skillful understatement. The flamboyant villainy goes to Dunaway, who depicts the frenzied female executive with all the drama of maniacal satire while Duvall's ruthless network executive is a blander, smoother type. Duvall said that he played Frank Hackett like "a vicious President Ford" (the film was released in 1976). Hackett, of course, doesn't see himself as a villain, but rather as a much put-upon executive having to deal with a "lunatic" like Beale, insubordinates like Schumacher, and the whims of a capricious boss. Duvall plays him with much constraint, not giving him too expressive a personality because the corporate henchman keeps a tight rein on himself. Dunaway's performance is studded with satirical gems like the way she rants about ratings while making love. Duvall manages to convey servility through a terse phone conversation with his boss, and ruthlessness through the way he fires the William Holden character with a rage that never gets out of hand.

Arch villains of melodrama are a lot easier to play than restrained ones like the hypocritical Major Burns or the unscrupulous Frank Hackett. Duvall makes them real because he makes them consistent and, thus, less blatant in their villainy and more complex in their characteristics and motivations.

Like *M*A*S*H*, *Network* was a film using bizarre situations to illustrate societal absurdities. Some critics found Sidney Lumet's direction too clumsy and Paddy Chayevsky's script too improbable—more like "social science fiction," as Richard Schickel put it in *Time*, than social satire.

Of the two films, it was *M*A*S*H* that had by far the greater impact, spinning off into one of TV's most celebrated and respected series, a symbol of the perpetual struggle against a timeless slaughter and bureaucracy. *Network*, rooted in the trends of the mid-seventies, has a dated flavor today despite the relevance of TV addiction. And while most of the audience may not remember that

Duvall was in either picture, they remember the characters that Duvall brought to life so skillfully.

Both roles contained a great deal of humor, but it was the humor of sophisticated satire, not of slapstick laughs and flashy caricatures. *M*A*S*H* and *Network* are excellent illustrations of Duvall's ability to blend into the movie he is making, to become the character he is portraying so totally that it is the character rather than the actor who is recalled later.

Duvall's chameleonlike quality opened doors for him that would have remained closed to a less adaptable performer. When director Herbert Ross approached Duvall about playing Dr. Watson in his forthcoming picture about Sherlock Holmes and Sigmund Freud, he was hesitant. His Hollywood friends were pointing out how formidable a task it would be for an American actor to hold his own in a cast composed of such British luminaries as Nicol Williamson and Vanessa Redgrave, not to mention the venerable Sir Laurence Olivier. But Ross was firm in his faith in Duvall's ability and persuaded him to make a tape as a kind of audition, which would be played for the English cast to see if the American could pull off the proper accent for *The Seven-Per-Cent Solution.*

He did. The tape was in the form of a conversation between Watson and the American interviewer, Paul Gleason:

> Gleason: *"Hey Doc, what's going on? Are you still working for old Holmes? There's a rumor floating around that he's gotten a little bit faggoty."*
> Watson: *"Holmes is not a homo. Holmes is man enough to enjoy a good woman."*

Duvall's tone was right off the playing fields of Eton. When the tape was played for the English cast they had to agree that the accent was pure enough by any standard. But

Duvall still wasn't satisfied, and he worked with a voice coach two hours a day for three weeks to perfect the clipped speech of the British upper classes. Despite the conformity of the accent, Duvall's Dr. Watson was a departure from the traditional depiction of the role.

"Dr. Watson, portrayed by Nigel Bruce for years as a doddering, well-meaning, generally ineffectual chap, is here interpreted by Robert Duvall in a much more interesting way—as a younger, more vigorous fellow with a pretty wife, a man capable of great empathy as he sees Holmes's suffering," Mort Sheinman wrote in *Women's Wear Daily*. Not everyone agreed with this assessment. Jay Cocks said in *Time* that "Duvall's Watson resembles a vaudeville Englishman, all jowls and bluster."

But the general consensus was otherwise, and Katie Kelly spoke for the great majority of critics when she wrote in the *East Side Express*, "The stand-out of the film was Robert Duvall as Dr. Watson. Duvall, as American as a hockey game, fit into that all-English landscape like a crumpet at a tea party."

Pauline Kael was equally emphatic in *The New Yorker:* "The fun of watching Robert Duvall as Doctor Watson is in his contrast to Nigel Bruce's bumble and, of course, in his new British accent."

Judith Crist was also impressed with Duvall's interpretation of Watson. In a review in *The Saturday Review* entitled "Sherlock Meets Sigmund in Lushest Vienna," she commented: "The cast is as urbane as the directorial tone. Nicol Williamson and Robert Duvall bring a refreshing vigor and muscularity to the Holmes-Watson screen tradition, with an interesting new emphasis on an equalitarian friendship between them."

The Seven-Per-Cent Solution was a demanding picture to play in because everyone involved with it was so terribly good at what they did. The screenplay was by Nicholas Meyer, author of the best-selling novel by the same name, who wrote a lavish period piece in which a cocaine-ravaged Sherlock Holmes is taken to a wise and humorous Sigmund Freud for treatment. It's a highly entertaining movie full of surprises, from Alan Arkin's delightfully engaging Freud, complete with beard and thick German accent, and Vanessa Redgrave as a beguiling damsel in distress, to Laurence Olivier as a timorous Professor Moriarty. Watching *The Seven-Per-Cent Solution* is so enjoyable that one gets a sense of just how much fun making it must have been.

Duvall relished the chance to work with such an illustrious collection of British performers and made the most of the opportunity to put his own stamp on such a well-known role as the ever-loyal Dr. Watson. Sporting a sandy-colored handlebar mustache, he emanates the stocky solidity that typified the upper-class Englishman in the plush 1890s. But his Watson is also a man of feelings, receptive to Freud's genius, sensitive to Holmes's anguish.

Dr. Watson was another part calling for restraint. Williamson was maniacal in his depiction of the later stages of cocaine addiction; Arkin was masterful as the kindly, brilliant Dr. Freud. Duvall's role is the background figure who reacts to the other two rather than initiating action of his own, his personality more muted, his mannerisms more subtle than theirs.

Duvall met the challenges offered by the Dr. Watson role with his usual thoroughness of detail and depth of comprehension of the character he's portraying. His Watson is as totally *decent* a human being as his TV executive in *Network* is loathsome. The two films were released the same year, 1976, and taken together they are a tribute to the incredible versatility of Robert Duvall.

In discussing Duvall's approach to acting, it's too easy to

sound academic about what is for him an intuitive process rather than a mental one. Although his technique sounds similar to the Method school of acting taught by Lee Strasberg at the Actors Studio, Duvall declines to identify himself with that approach. A maverick by nature, he resists attempts to neatly categorize him. Another reason for his dislike of being labeled a Method actor may be that Strasberg's classes were always heavy on psychoanalytic interpretation, with exhaustive discussions of motivation following scenes presented by students. Duvall has never been inclined to wallow in such introspective waters.

In an unusually candid interview with Paul Gleason for *Club* magazine, Duvall said he was convinced analysis would not be an asset to his acting ability. "You may get to know yourself better, but how are you going to necessarily tap impulses better if you know yourself mentally better? I know things that'll set me off and how to use them, but at the outset I like to go intuitive. I don't like to become too mental anyway. I like to go instinctively in a part."

Duvall will tackle a new role by his brand of behavorial research, observing the mannerisms and speech of people similar to the character he's playing, and by the kind of historical research he did for his portrayal of Jesse James. Then he'll piece together a composite character sketch from his observations and studies. Next, he reaches down somewhere deep inside himself and finds something of the character he's playing within him. But it's not a process he's comfortable verbalizing.

Like all true art processes, Duvall's rare talent for bringing a character to life remains something of a mystery to others—and probably to himself as well. He hangs around a guy's memories and and then something happens when he's in front of a camera or a live audience, and that something is art that defies definition. The more appropriate response to a Robert Duvall performance is not analysis of its component parts, but awe at the beauty of the whole.

5

THE
FAULKNERIAN FARMER
AND THE METHODICAL MAFIOSO

Two movies in which Robert Duvall played were released in 1972 and were as far apart as products of the same medium can be. One of them opened in a simultaneous premiere engagment at five midtown Manhattan theaters. It grossed a million dollars a day in its first month. After two years it had grossed a record-breaking $330,000,000 and was sold to television for an unprecedented $10,000,000. It was produced by the powerful Paramount Pictures, was directed by a mercurial young cinematic genius, and starred the country's most famous actor. It was called *The Godfather*.

The other movie cost $400,000 to make and didn't gross too much more than that. It was produced by an obscure company, and no one in its cast was particularly well-known at the time. It received some favorable critical attention, but was virtually ignored at the box office. It was called *Tomorrow*.

Of the two movies, Robert Duvall's favorite was *Tomorrow*.

He has always believed that his portrayal of *Tomorrow*'s homespun hero, the semiretarded dirt farmer Jackson Fentry, represents his greatest triumph. The movie was also a source of chagrin to Duvall because of the frustrations inherent in being involved in a creative endeavor over which he had no ultimate control. When it came down to the wire, or the cutting room floor, the producers had the final say.

Gilbert Pearlman and Paul Roebling were intent on making a movie of the highest quality. But it was inevitable that they would clash with the feisty actor because the project struck such a deep nerve in him. It was one of those rare low-budget, independently produced films that attract a wealth of talent. *Tomorrow* was originally a short story by William Faulkner, one of America's foremost writers and winner of both the Nobel and Pulitzer Prizes, whose chronicles of Southern life rank with the greatest literature of the century.

The screenplay was by Horton Foote, an artist as steeped in Southern identity as Faulkner himself. Foote had won an Academy Award for his film adaptation of *To Kill a Mockingbird*. Then he had seen an original work of his, *The Chase*, butchered by Hollywood's excesses and extravagances. Foote first adapted the Faulkner story into dramatic form not for the movies at all, but for TV's "Playhouse 90." When he expanded it into a full-length script for the Playwrights Foundation, it was performed for a few weeks in 1968 at the Herbert Berghof Studio. Foote chose Duvall to play Fentry and the stage actress Olga Bellin to play Sarah Eubanks, the woman he loves in adversity and loses to death.

Jackson was like a continuation of the Boo Radley role, as though Boo had been given a voice and center stage. From the beginning Duvall felt a strong affinity for the character. That first night on the Berghof stage was one of the highs of his life. *Midnight Cowboy* was being filmed nearby; Dustin Hoffman and Jon Voight were in the audience. "It was a great evening," Duvall recalls with relish. "It's like an athletic event—I was so up. When I opened my mouth with that accent, I could hear Dusty roar, 'Whoo! Whoo!' It was like an electrical evening. . . . Everything caught right and after it they were bravoing, schtomping, standing. . . ."

The memory of that stirring connection with the audience stayed with Duvall. When the offer came to bring Jackson Fentry to the screen, opposite Olga Bellin again, and again with a Horton Foote script, he saw the opportunity to make a uniquely honest movie about that region of the country he knew so well and those people he respected so much. Foote shared Duvall's vision, which made them natural allies in the struggle for authenticity.

The pair of them held out against the producers' initial plan to shoot the film in Hollywood. The director, Joseph Anthony, a sensitive moviemaker who had directed *The Rainmaker* and *The Matchmaker*, suggested a Connecticut location. But Duvall and Foote wouldn't give in. They insisted on a Mississippi location—and they finally won out.

Elated, Duvall got in his Volkswagen and drove down to Mississippi, roaming the countryside near the Arkansas border, talking to the local people, taping their speech to perfect his Fentry accent, reading up on county history. He bought the battered coat he wears in the movie for five dollars from a black man standing on the side of the road in Ripley, Mississippi, on a "First Monday," the day of the month set aside for bartering knives, guns, and hunting dogs. For the cap Fentry wears, Duvall went to a railroad engineer and asked to buy the one on his head; the man refused to sell it to him, but gladly made him a present of it.

When the location was set up in the small town of Tupelo, the cast and crew immersed themselves in the local life. Instead of having their food shipped in, the producers arranged for the women in the town to provide it. Those ladies turned out to have a very competitive spirit, each trying to outdo the others in heaping fowl, ham, steak, fish, vegetables, homemade bread with fresh butter, honey, pies, and mouth-watering cakes on their visitors.

Duvall and Foote encouraged Pearlman and Roebling to

hire local people for the bit parts. In casting Fentry's foster son, Jackson Longstreet, they chose not a Hollywood prodigy, but a boy from nearby Possum Trot who had been an incubator baby and was at age seven small enough to play a four-year-old. Duvall established a relationship with him by talking in phrases familiar to the child. Knowing that Southern men, when they want affection from a kid or a dog, say, "Love muh neck," he would whisper those words to Johnny Mask, and receive in response a big kiss on the neck.

Duvall lost twenty pounds and lined his face to look gaunt and drawn. He poured the best of his creative energies into this picture. He had long been convinced that Hollywood knew nothing of this kind of people, that their only guideline for depicting them came from other movies. He felt it was essential that the picture be true to the way of life and behavior of the people it depicted. His trust in Foote was total; with everyone else he was somewhat skeptical.

He couldn't have been easy to work with because he was so sure of exactly what he wanted in this picture. It would have been an impossible situation were he working with an overbearing director. But Joseph Anthony had a subtle touch and gave the actor a lot of freedom to develop his part. Still, there were problems. Anthony, when asked by a friend how Duvall was to work with, replied, "Difficult. Very difficult." There was tension with the producers, too, and Duvall extracted from them the promise that he be allowed in the cutting room and have a say in the editing decisions.

Despite all the conflicts, a remarkable movie was made in that Mississippi town. It is centered on Jackson Fentry, whose story is told in flashbacks through the voice-over of a puzzled lawyer who can't understand why a weather-beaten dirt farmer has hung a jury about to acquit a man of killing a no-good roughneck. The answer goes back about twenty years to the winter that farmer took a job as a watchman at an unused sawmill. The day before Christmas Jackson's life is irrevocably changed when Sarah Eubanks turns up at his door pregnant, abandoned, and thoroughly worn out. Fentry takes her in and cares for her until her baby is born. She dies shortly after the birth; grief-stricken, Fentry assumes responsibility for the baby boy.

The farmer pours all the love Sarah has kindled in him into her child. We see him picking cotton with the baby strapped to his back, lifting the toddler in and out of his wagon, his tenderness for the boy permeating his every gesture. This idyll is shattered when Sarah's brothers suddenly turn up, demanding their kin. The law is on their side, and, once again, Jackson Fentry loses what he loves most. Years later the boy turns up in the town again, a troublemaker who's killed in a fight he starts. But juryman Jackson Fentry will not acquit the defendant who took the life of the man who was once, for a tragically brief time, his son.

Duvall's portrayal of Jackson Fentry was a deeply satisfying one. If Eddie Carbone in *A View from the Bridge* was his Othello, then the lonely farmer, he has said, was his King Lear. But gratifying as the role was to him, the movie still had its disappointments. He found that even an independent production doesn't guarantee artistic autonomy, that "the power still lies with the producer and the cutter." Some of Duvall's favorite scenes were cut, and they almost cut one that he felt was crucial to his characterization. It's Fentry's speech given immediately after Sarah dies. Duvall was incensed at this omission and resolved to do something about it. Hurriedly, he put in a phone call to Horton Foote at his New Hampshire home, urging the playwright to use his influence to save the scene. Foote's intervention was successful, but the cuts were still a source of discontent for Duvall. So were the reviews, which were very mixed.

Many a critic's customary reserve was melted down by the force of the film's emotional impact. Sheila Benson wrote in the *Los Angeles Times,* ". . . if you can take your eyes from the screen, look around the theater at the faces of others watching as Jackson Fentry is described as 'the lowly and the invincible of the earth,' who have the quality 'to endure and endure, and then endure. Tomorrow, and tomorrow, and tomorrow.' Your tears have a room full of company." Another who was deeply moved was Judith Crist, who in her *New York* magazine review said that Duvall and Bellin "create those lives with an insight that is devastating. Theirs is a duet beyond compare, an offering of such subtlety that it glows—and grows—in retrospect."

"Sublime" was Gene Shalit's word for Duvall's performance. But there were other reactions. Jay Cocks in his *Time* review found Foote's screenplay "mawkish" and Alan Green's camera lacking "in all tone except a flat, relentless gray." Penelope Gilliatt said in *The New Yorker* that there was "a monotony about the whole film," attributable to the rhythm of the direction, which distributes too many pauses between dialogue lines.

Vincent Canby was also disturbed by the slow pace of the film. He wrote in *The New York Times* that "Jackson Fentry is a young Mississippi cotton farmer who is so taciturn that he almost seems catatonic. . . . When he does talk, however, something very peculiar happens, but I'm not sure whether it's because of the dialogue given him, the cracker accent he affects, or perhaps the bad balance of a postsychronized sound track. Whatever the reason, the voice sounds as if it had been supplied by a ventriloquist. Even if the movie's intentions are decent, as reflected in the accurate look of the production, filmed in Mississippi, the effect is mostly patronizing."

Duvall, infuriated by criticisms of his so carefully studied

Fentry accent, claimed that New York critics had no idea how people west of New Jersey talk. He also felt that the picture was poorly distributed by the producers. However, given the reality of popular taste, a film like *Tomorrow* is not a picture likely to have a mass appeal even with the most zealous distribution.

Although *Tomorrow* was not widely distributed, Duvall was getting a good amount of exposure in 1972 because he was in four films released that year. Those whose tastes ran to the quieter, more serious film could ferret out *Tomorrow* and see Duvall as the gaunt dirt farmer. Clint Eastwood fans who flocked to the Western *Joe Kidd* got to see Duvall playing a low-down, mean landowner. In another kind of Western, he could be seen as the psychotic, fanatical Jesse James with a zany bowl haircut and a crazy air about him in that new look at an old legend, *The Great Northfield Minnesota Raid*.

And there was *The Godfather*. A universe away from Jackson Fentry with his tattered clothes and haggard face was Tom Hagen, the don's foster son and legal counselor, the Corleone family's most trusted adviser despite his non-Italian origin, the *consigliere*. Conservatively dressed and immaculately groomed, he moves smoothly and unobtrusively through dimly lit interiors; fair-haired and calm, he is always a contrast to the swarthy, volatile men around him. Carefully positioned to whisper into the ear of his don, he offers his calculated advice, his legal expertise, in clipped low tones. Tom Hagen carries out his duties with a steely composure, his loyalty unquestioned in a world where nothing is taken for granted, his devotion and dedication absolute, while his ruthlessness is lurking just beneath his urbane veneer.

Working on *The Godfather* was an interesting experience, if only for the intrigues and tensions generated by Coppola's struggle for creative autonomy. The Paramount powers were wary of the fiery director whose track record at thirty-two showed three previous films, none of them successful. Bob Evans, the executive producer who believed in Coppola enough to hire him over considerable opposition, still wasn't sure of his choice and so had an understudy director on the set following Coppola around should Evans change his mind. Duvall's sympathies were all with Coppola, of course, knowing all too well what losing creative control can do to an artistic spirit. He had liked working with Coppola on *The Rain People* and was pleased to see that even on the set of *The Godfather,* where the stakes were so much higher, the egomaniacal director had the sense to give his cast considerable leeway in interpreting their parts.

The prospect of working with Brando, the idol of a generation of actors, had everyone all keyed up. Before the shooting began, the cast met for a lavish dinner at Patsy's, a trendy New York Italian restaurant.

"Everyone was nervous about meeting Marlon Brando and immediately started relating to him as the Godfather," Coppola recalls with fond amusement. "Jimmy Caan started telling jokes, Al Pacino looked tragic, and every time Marlon Brando turned his back, Bobby Duvall started imitating him."

Duvall had found Brando aloof when they worked together on *The Chase.* But this time the star, while still keeping pretty much to himself, was more accessible, even joining in with some of the clowning Caan and Duvall loved to do whenever they found themselves working on the same picture. The two of them did a lot of mooning at inopportune moments and soon had Brando engaging in that activity himself. This glimpse of a more human Brando did nothing to diminish his status in the eyes of Duvall, who found him incomparable in his "inner power and a certain brilliant intensity."

It was Coppola who had first realized that the then forty-five-year-old Brando could be convincing as the sixty-five-year-old Don Corleone. To persuade Paramount of this, Coppola had the studio honchos watch a screen test of an anonymous but familiar actor—Marlon Brando in full God-father makeup. His cheeks puffed out to jowls, his eyes shadowed, his throat and neck wrinkled, his voice hoarse and wary, his gestures cautious and deliberate, Brando *was* the elderly Vito Corleone.

Coppola kept having hassles with Paramount over the casting. He wanted the five-foot-seven-inch, Bronx-bred Al Pacino to play Vito Corleone's youngest son, Michael, the character on whom the film is most extensively focused. The studio disagreed with this choice, and Pacino had already signed to do *The Gang That Couldn't Shoot Straight* when they changed their minds, leaving the actor to get out of that contract. After months of expensive screen tests, Paramount came up with the cast Coppola had asked for in the beginning. With his accurate casting intuition, the em-battled director knew Pacino had not only that dark, intense look so suggestive of Dustin Hoffman, but also the talent to portray the corruption of an idealistic youth as he assumes power. And he knew that Brando had the presence to con-vey the elderly don's strength and intractable will.

Brando had a lot of input into the image his character projected and wouldn't let him be seen in any but a sympa-thetic light. In a scene with Duvall, Brando flatly refused to say the lines of a cynical old man telling his young lawyer, "A man with a briefcase can steal more than a hundred men with guns." Brando, Duvall noticed, "wanted the guy to be a saint."

This tendency of the film to romanticize the Mafia—a name never used in the movie—disturbed many of the critics even while they admitted that the picture offered deeply engrossing entertainment. Nobody immediately connected with the project seems to have had any firsthand knowledge of the mob. Mario Puzo, whose first two novels didn't make him any money, sat down to write a best-seller and turned out *The Godfather* based on ethnic gossip and mythology about crime kings. Paramount trusted his instincts enough to finance the writing of the book, which eventually sold 500,000 hardcover copies and 10,000,000 paperbacks.

Puzo and Coppola wrote the screenplay together. Coppola needed money to make the experimental films he wanted to be doing. He didn't know anything more about how real gangsters behave than Puzo did, but he possessed a very colorful imagination, and a decidedly romantic one. Coppola didn't set out to romanticize the Mafia; he was caught up in making an emotionally gripping, vastly absorbing film about a fictional family of criminals who may or may not have resembled actual ones. *Life*'s savvy critic Richard Schickel was well aware of this intent, and of how well Coppola had pulled it off, when he wrote of the director's touch, "Everything he shows us—the faces of the mobsters and their loved ones, the furnishings of their home, the very pasta on their tables—looks and feels right. And that dumb-shrewd, tough-tender dialogue. If real hoods don't talk this way, they ought to."

The only one who actually bothered to find out how real hoods talk was Duvall. Through an old friend from East Harlem, he met a few examples of the real thing and quickly picked up a lot not only about their style, but also about their personalities. "They admit they're hoods," he says of those unsavory subjects of his research, "they joke about it, but there's a real viciousness underneath it with every one of them." And it was that real viciousness, Duvall realized, that Brando, who wanted to play a totally sympathetic role, and Coppola with his romantic approach, wouldn't portray in their picture.

Digging deeper into mob mores to better understand what makes a Tom Hagen tick, Duvall learned about the Mafia concept of "respect," about the deference a younger man shows for an older, more powerful one. He came to see that Hagen was a glorified gofer, obediently doing his master's bidding while retaining his pride and maintaining his position. "It was," Duvall realized, "a touchy thing. He had to ride on the periphery. You couldn't step in, as either the character or the actor. You always had to step back." And no actor could step back with more finesse than Robert Duvall.

In building his Tom Hagen role, Duvall gave his customary attention to each detail that was the raw material out of which he would sculpt the character he would bring to life in front of the camera. He strove to convey the contradictions in this man whose legal education was superimposed on his native street smarts. His Hagen accent is reflective of this duality in the character. Duvall acquired the speech pattern of an Irish-American New Yorker who has gone to one of the city's Catholic law schools, perhaps Fordham or St. John's, but who has kept something of the streets in the way he talks. Putting all the Tom Hagen pieces together, Duvall gave a performance whose astuteness was noticed by those discerning enough to see how germane it was to the film's theme.

Writing in *Academy Awards: Oscar Annual* (1973), Robert Osborne explained that Tom Hagen was "one of *The Godfather*'s least showy, most important roles. . . . More than any other character in the massive saga, he expressed the film's concept of the Mafia as a corporate business run methodically and matter-of-factly, as if it were dealing in daily matters such as stocks and bonds rather than gangland gunnings and cold-blooded murders. Robert Duvall played Hagen low-key, loyal, an eye always on business, efficiently carrying out his duties with a minimum of waves; it was a powerful performance [that] added immeasurably to the film."

The Godfather brought Duvall a recognition he hadn't experienced before. His portrayal of the Corleones' *consigliere* won him an Academy Award nomination and a New York Film Critics Award for best supporting actor. He was offered the lead in *Badge 373,* a percentage of its net profits, and such fringe benefits as an expense account and a room in a first-class hotel so that he could stay in the city during the shooting instead of having to commute to Tuxedo Park daily.

Now he was gaining weight to look like Eddie Egan as assiduously as he had shed pounds for the gaunt appearance of Jackson Fentry. Nor did he wear his Tom Hagen hairpiece, because he thought the scruffy detective should be balding. Duvall wasn't the only actor from *The Godfather* playing a cop; Al Pacino went from the featured role of the scion of a criminal dynasty in *The Godfather* to the starring one in *Serpico,* a fast-paced story about an incorruptible young detective.

The Godfather, though, was not a thing of the past. The mafioso movie had outgrossed even the all-time record-breaker, *Gone With the Wind,* and the studio would be pleased to see a sequel. Coppola was convinced he could deliver one; from the leftovers of Puzo's novel that he hadn't been able to squeeze into the first movie, he could make a second.

Everyone would be earning a lot more money this time around. Duvall, who had been on straight salary for the first, was offered a percentage of *Part II*. It was an offer he couldn't refuse, especially since he would be playing a role he'd developed himself and had Coppola's assurance that this new project would be a significant film, not the cheap knock-off sequels often are.

This new movie was much more in Coppola's hands from the outset than the first one had been. Not only was he writing the script from Puzo's treatment and first-draft screenplay, and, of course, directing the film; he was also producing it. Coppola's stock with the studio had gone way up since Bob Evans had had a possible replacement stalking him on the set in case he didn't work out. The producer-director-scriptwriter was allowed to do his own casting, but the usual wrestle for control took place when it was time for the cutting. Coppola always felt that his three-hour opus suffered from being too severely cut, while Bob Evans would claim that he had had to strenuously cut and edit the sequel to get it into any kind of viewing shape because Coppola had left it in such a chaotic state. Evans went so far as to blame the breakup of his marriage on the film, complaining that when his then-wife Ali McGraw was making *The Getaway* with Steve McQueen, for whom she left him, he was too busy with *The Godfather, Part II,* to visit her on location.

Godfather II was a more lavish production than its extravagant predecessor. Coppola sardonically referred to the sequel as a $13 million art form. While the first closely followed the Puzo novel, telling the story of Michael Corleone from the mid-forties to the mid-fifties as he is transformed from an idealistic young man living outside his family's orbit into the new godfather, *Part II* spans six decades and jumps from Sicily to Lake Tahoe to Cuba. The film is a series of crosscuts juxtaposing the story of Vito Corleone's rise in the ranks of organized crime to Michael's fall into an abyss of corruption and paranoia from which there is no escape.

Although the first part's plot had been centered on Michael, it was the Vito Corleone/Marlon Brando aura that dominated the picture. Now the focus was divided between Al Pacino, who continued his sensitive portrayal of Michael, and Robert De Niro, who played the young Vito.

De Niro had been featured in Martin Scorsese's *Mean Streets,* a searing look at the styles and compromises of life in contemporary Little Italy. Now he was cast in that same setting seven decades earlier. The son of artists, De Niro had grown up on the streets of Greenwich Village and had done his share of workshop productions, off-off-Broadway plays, dinner theaters, and touring companies for long years before the starring roles came his way.

In De Niro and Pacino, Duvall saw an intensity to match his own. He was several years older, but they were of the same generation when it came to their histories and lifestyles. They were all New York actors, a term loosely used to describe a mentality of dedication, stage-oriented techniques, and impoverished apprenticeships.

De Niro approached the demanding task of following in Brando's footsteps with what his friends saw as his demonic, obsessive, and perfectionistic attitude about his work. The critics were amazed at how skillfully De Niro took the characteristics Brando had exhibited as the elderly Don Corleone and put them into the much younger Vito, making the alterations time would have made, but in reverse. De Niro's Vito and Pacino's Michael perfectly complement each other because the young Vito is, as Pauline Kael put it, "secure in the knowledge of how dangerous he is . . . his courtliness is a noblesse oblige," while Michael is "sullen and withdrawn."

Vincent Canby took exception to this contrast between

the Corleones' past and present. "The idea that old-time criminals were somehow less vicious and venal than today's is as romantic as any notion that turned up in the original film," he wrote in his *Times* review. Others, like Emily Genauer in the *New York Post,* maintained that *Godfather II*'s portrait of a "human corruption so total as to corrode governments and a whole society" was ample correction of any whitewash of the mob the first *Godfather* may have inadvertently contained.

Besides this debate over Coppola's interpretation of crime in twentieth-century America, the critics were divided about the form of the film. Some found it a brilliantly conceived epic, while others saw it as more fragmented than sprawling, more tedious than comprehensive. Whatever their disagreements over questions of the picture's theme and structure, the critics were united in their enthusiasm for the acting. There was praise for De Niro's finely tuned portrait of what was in essence a young Marlon Brando. One reviewer noted that so flawless was De Niro's depiction of the young Vito that he spoke the Sicilian dialect he'd learned for the part with ease, while his English had the cautious hesitancy of the nonnative speaker.

There were kudos for Al Pacino, who in the course of the two films traveled the road from sympathetic to sinister character with admirable skill. It was Pacino, a member of the Actors Studio, who persuaded its legendary director, Lee Strasberg, to play the part of Hyman Roth, a Meyer Lansky-like gangster. The cast was fascinated by Brando's teacher, the renowned master of the Method, in his first screen role ever and his first acting one since he played in a Clifford Odets one-act piece in the 1930s. Strasberg spent weeks before the shooting living the part of the frail, aged, but still tough-as-nails mobster until, he said, even his wife scarcely knew him. At seventy-three, Strasberg faced the camera for the first time and gave a magnificent performance as the ailing but implacable man who beneath his fussy pleasantries won't yield an inch.

"Even his breath control is impeccable," Pauline Kael said of Strasberg's depiction of his character's physical infirmities. She also had some fine praise for Duvall in her highly respected *New Yorker* review: "As the bland, despicably loyal Tom Hagen, more square-faced and sturdy now, Robert Duvall, a powerful recessive actor, is practically a genius at keeping himself in the background."

She noticed. And *Godfather II* would be an easy movie to get lost in. The sheer vastness of its scope, from Sicilian vendettas to revolution in Cuba, and all the intrigues and bloodshed in between, could easily overshadow all but its two leads. But Duvall attracted attention simply by the talent with which he stayed unobtrusive. He's even more of a background figure in *Part II* than in the first part because the settings are so much more far-flung. In *The Godfather,* the action is more centered on the family's home, where Tom Hagen is a constant figure. But when he is on screen in the sequel, he provides a welcome continuity, a much-needed bridge between the two films. The similarity of his behavior to Vito Corleone in the first part and to Michael Corleone in *Part II* is symbolic of how the mantle of leadership has been passed from father to son.

The Godfather, Part II, won seven Oscars, including Best Picture, Best Supporting Actor for De Niro, and Best Director for the indefatigable Francis Coppola, who a few years later edited both parts into chronological order for television. The Corleone saga passed into the American consciousness; for better or worse, it became the great American epic in which the gangsters ultimately were transformed into symbols of greed, corruption, and perversion of the American dream. It also brought the features of everyone with an important role in the film firmly into the public's mind.

Despite the boost *The Godfather* epic gave to his career, Duvall's feelings about the films have always been ambivalent. A few years after the completion of *Part II*, Duvall told interviewer Paul Gleason that while *The Godfather* had put him in the position where he was offered leads, he'd just as soon have the main supporting role unless the lead was a really interesting part. "I had a good career before [*The Godfather*] and I would always have a good career regardless of *The Godfather*. I got the part in *The Seven-Per-Cent Solution,* and that had nothing to do with *The Godfather.*"

His reluctance to attribute his subsequent success to that controversial blockbuster probably stems from pride not only in his work, but also in how he was going about developing his career—not trying for an instant push to the top, but building, role upon role, his reputation as a versatile actor of the highest quality. And his reactions to the epic that was so helpful to that reputation remained mixed. The actor in Duvall fully understood that with a director as romantic in his vision as Coppola, and a cast as appealing as Marlon Brando, Al Pacino, Robert De Niro, and James Caan, the result was bound to be characterizations sympathetic to the point of idealization. The actor understood; but the man of principle was never comfortable with it.

Duvall takes exception to a line of Michael Corleone's in *Part II* that the head of a criminal organization is no different from the head of Du Pont. "That's a little naive, I think. I mean, Jimmy Hoffa is in the ground. You lose your job or your wits working for a big company, but I don't think you're gonna get killed if you go one-to-one against the head of Du Pont." He was hitting on a basic flaw in the movie's ideology that was also disturbing to a serious thinker like Stanley Kauffmann, *The New Republic*'s film critic, who wrote of his objection to *The Godfather*'s "adolescent implication of analogy between the Mafia and corporate capitalism."

Duvall once made the following thoughtful comment to an interviewer asking him about *The Godfather:* "I talked to an undertaker. He said one time, with a suicide—guy put a .22 slug into his temple—he had to have somebody show him where the hole was. There was no blood. In films, no matter where you're hit, they have blood spurtin' out—a certain kind of way to romanticize crime. I think *Godfather* was a great film, brilliant director, but, I think, the tendency was to romanticize."

It remained a deep source of disappointment to Duvall that so few people got to see him in that quiet little film released the same year as the blockbuster. *The Godfather* helped him financially—no small thing to a man with a large country home replete with dogs, horses, and a private tennis court, as well as two teenaged girls in private school. It gave him more visibility, which led to offers of larger parts for more lucrative pay.

But it didn't touch his soul. His admiration for Coppola's creative genius was very strong, but the vision of the two movies belonged to the director, not to the actor who had so many reservations about the morality of their themes.

Duvall's personal vision lay elsewhere, back in the low-budget production about which the critics were divided and that most of the public never saw. *Tomorrow* was the film in which Robert Duvall passionately believed. Almost ten years went by between the filming of *To Kill a Mockingbird* and *Tomorrow*, and that many would pass before the next time Duvall played a similar role, Mac Sledge in *Tender Mercies*. Boo Radley, Jackson Fentry, and Mac Sledge all come out of Southern soil and are sunk in a lonely isolation, and to each is revealed the redeeming power of love. Each of these inarticulate but so emotionally expressive characters bears the stamp of Duvall's perception of the world.

Even those moviegoers who saw both *The Godfather* and *Tomorrow* may well not have realized that they were watching the same actor when they saw the efficient lawyer and the haggard farmer. The two are simply not recognizable as the same person. It's not just the world of difference between the styles of the two films, or the makeup, or even the accents.

Those things are there, but there's also something more. There is nothing of the ruthless, controlled Tom Hagen in the silently suffering Jackson Fentry, nothing of Fentry's depth of compassion in Hagen's cold competence. The two men don't connect at any point whatsoever. And Duvall's performance was so true to each of them that even he doesn't exist as a bridge between them.

That Duvall could so thoroughly realize two such disparate characters as those he played in *Tomorrow* and *The Godfather* is a tribute to the actor's versatility; that he prefers his portrayal of the cotton farmer to the *consigliere* is a reflection of the man's values. It shows where his roots lie, who his heroes are, and what style of motion picture production he most indentifies with.

6

THOSE MACHO
FIGHTING MACHINES

"I love the smell of napalm in the morning. . . . It smells like victory." That exuberantly delivered line from the far side of sanity comes from Duvall, playing Lieutenant Colonel Kilgore in Coppola's Vietnam extravaganza, *Apocalypse Now.*

Against a dawn-streaked sky the choppers swoop down on a coastal village, their PA's blaring Wagner's exultant "Ride of the Valkyries." Their arrival is greeted by a burst of Viet Cong shells. While his terrified men scramble for shelter, Kilgore remains upright. The surfboard attached to his helicopter bespeaks the crucial nature of his mission: Kilgore is going surfing.

"What do you know about surfing, Captain? You're from New Jersey," he counters an objection to this senseless raid. He's crazed, this Kilgore, but there's an exuberance to his maniacal energy that does a lot to explain how a man gets high on war. It would have been easy to play Kilgore as satire, as blatant caricature, but Duvall didn't. What's most frightening about this napalm-happy, surf-loving fanatic is that he seems real.

"If what Kilgore does in the film is absurd, then the absurdity lies in the reality," Duvall said of the madcap air cavalry officer. The reality is the madness that was Vietnam. Coppola spent $30 million trying to capture that mood on the screen, and in his few brief scenes Duvall sums it up more memorably than at any other point in the movie. Ask anybody today to quote any lines from Marlon Brando's bloated, unhinged Green Beret turned mystic, or the picture's protagonist, Martin Sheen's battle-scarred Captain Willard, and you draw a blank. But Kilgore's napalm in the morning line: Is there anyone who saw the movie who doesn't vividly recall it?

It's that same ability to extract Coppola's theme from the trappings of a lavish production and then illustrate it with absolute clarity that Duvall demonstrated in *The Godfather*. As he earned critical praise in the earlier epic for personifying the cutthroat gangster turned corporate wheeler-dealer, so in the Vietnam saga he received popular acclaim for personifying the bizarre and macabre aspects of an era in the role of the freaky Kilgore.

Building the Kilgore character, Duvall, as always, went in search of the source. Spending time with air cavalry men, he hung around their memories long enough to understand that their identities were rooted in the traditions of the old cavalry, when men still fought on horseback; hence Kilgore's spurs and the crossed swords on his black broad-brimmed hat. He also learned that many of them *had* actually strapped surfboards to their choppers so that they could go surfing when they weren't fighting.

Digging up memories of Special Services men he'd known in the Army, Duvall added them to his composite character. Then he took these real-life men, twisted their dedication to battle, perverted their passion for flamboyant traditions, and filled in the fanatical features of Kilgore. And there was another person on whom he modeled the mad flyer—Francis Coppola. In Kilgore's last scene he becomes enraged that the surf is messed up. When Coppola yelled "Action!" Duvall threw the megaphone he was holding up in the air and walked away. After the scene was shot, the director rushed up to the actor, wanting to know how he'd thought up that terrifically expressive gesture.

"I was just playing you in one of your tantrums," Duvall replied.

The Kilgore role got so embedded in Duvall that it enabled him to overcome the fear of heights he'd had for as long as he could remember. The script called for him to lean out of an airplane 1,500 feet above ground to drop a grenade. Less than a year earlier, while making *The Killer Elite* in San Francisco under Sam Peckinpah's direction, Duvall had thrown rocks at the camera and stalked off the set when asked to walk along the ledge of a roof without a railing. Now Coppola was yelling "Lean out, damn it!" while shooting the plane scene. Duvall—or the Kilgore in Duvall—leaned out.

A lot of people working on *Apocalypse Now* were seeing changes in themselves as they got caught up in the hysteria of making that extraordinary picture. From the beginning, it was Coppola's vision. This time there would be no studio executives between the director and his dream. The movie was Coppola's property from the start, produced by his own company, Zoetrope, and financed by preselling distribution rights to United Artists and to foreign countries. The budget was originally set at $14 million. When the film ended up costing over twice that, Coppola had to stake his entire personal fortune on its success.

Coppola wanted visual imagery and special effects such as had never been seen before. To that end, he hired Bernardo Bertolucci's cinematographer, Vittorio Storaro—a daring step because Europeans were used to working so differently from Americans, shooting frame by frame rather than a whole scene at once. Storaro turned out to be as much of a perfectionist as Coppola, and between them they created a movie of such stunningly spectacular visuals that it dazzled even those who were most critical of its content.

Coppola wrote the screenplay with the aid of John Milius, a brilliant young director who was a part of the experimental school of moviemakers centered around the San Francisco-based Zoetrope enterprise. Kilgore's attack on the coastal village was Milius's inspiration; and it was Storaro's cinematic genius that created those images of the choppers swooping down, incinerating the shoreline with napalm—a scene whose physical beauty was matched only by its moral savagery.

Adamant about attaining the best facsimile to the Vietnamese jungle he could find, Coppola chose a location in the Philippines that possessed a similar terrain. He planned to spend six months there and ended up spending sixteen. In his late thirties, but still regarded as Hollywood's bearded wunderkind, Coppola couldn't stop shooting scenes, spending money, writing and rewriting—sometimes whole scenes between takes—to capture on film the essence of the Vietnam experience. But it kept eluding him.

A myriad of disasters dogged his footsteps. He borrowed American aircraft and pilots from the Philippine Air Force, only to lose them for days as both pilots and planes were pressed into service to fight the rebels in the hills. A typhoon destroyed much of his set; Martin Sheen suffered a heart attack and was out of the shooting for more long weeks; Marlon Brando turned up in Manila grossly overweight to play the renegade Colonel Kurtz, and the director-screenwriter had to rethink his whole conception of the character to work around the unexpected extra poundage.

The episodes in the filming were becoming as bizarre as the experiences they was dramatizing. Villages were hastily constructed and then destroyed by explosives; a huge stone temple was built by 700 laborers and then demolished; expensive equipment disappeared in the mud; members of a primitive native tribe were brought onto the set as extras and lived there, holding ritual ceremonies that were incorporated into the movie.

When the dramatic incidents surrounding the making of the film came to rival those it was chronicling, Coppola was wracked by self-doubts. He was using as source material Joseph Conrad's short novel *Heart of Darkness,* in which a humanitarian, scholarly Belgian ivory agent drifts away from civilization into the savagery of the jungle. In Coppola's version Kurtz has managed to escape from the savagery of a civilization responsible for the Vietnam carnage into the Cambodian jungle, where he wages a war of his own, leading tribal soldiers, though for what and against whom is unclear.

Coppola was trying to film two journeys: the external one Captain Willard, who has been sent on a mission to find Kurtz and "terminate" him, undertakes as he leads a river patrol-boat expedition into Cambodia; and the internal one Willard undergoes as he starts to question everything in which he once believed. Willard's conflicts were reflected in Coppola's, who was no longer sure he was capable of getting his vision down on film and then shaping that footage into a coherent movie.

Duvall was hardly participating in the director's angst. In the spring of 1976 he spent two months on Baler Beach at the Philippine location, living in a cozy little hut, swimming in a nearby muddy river, and keeping in shape for Kilgore's lean, muscular look, an effort made easier by the fact that he couldn't stand the food served to the cast and crew, referring to it as "slop." Tanned and wearing the crew-cut hairpiece he used in the movie, he was in fine form on the set. Extolling the life of the second leading man, Duvall called it "the best in the world, because you travel and have a per diem, and probably a better part, plus you don't have the weight of the entire movie on your shoulders."

That weight was resting heavily on Coppola, who continued his pursuit of his Conrad metaphor despite every obstacle the jungle put in his path. What for the director was an undertaking threatening to tear apart the fabric of his life and his belief in himself was for Duvall a pleasant interlude in an exotic location, playing a part he thoroughly enjoyed. The irony is that it was Duvall who best captured the exuberance and insanity of fighting men that kept eluding Coppola.

Leaving the chaos of Coppola's set, Duvall took off for England, where he was to play another kind of fighting man—a German intelligence officer in the World War II adventure fantasy *The Eagle Has Landed*. The script was written by Tom Mankiewicz, author of three of the most successful James Bond pictures, and was adapted from the Jack Higgins novel about an attempt by Nazi agents to kidnap Winston Churchill. It was an elaborate production, shot on location in Finland, in London, on the Norfolk and Cornish coasts, and in a tiny village in the English countryside, and utilizing six German wartime aircraft still in good flying condition.

But it didn't work. The critics found the plot absurd and the actors badly miscast, with Michael Caine playing a German colonel who was too good to be true, Donald Sutherland as an Anglophilic Irish patriot, and Duvall as Colonel Max Rudl, who masterminds the ridiculously improbable scheme. Among the generally unfavorable reviews, including many scornful of the bad taste in making the Nazi officers such implausibly sympathetic characters, was praise for Duvall's effective German accent and makeup job.

The New Republic's Stanley Kauffmann took the opportunity of his negative review of the movie to say some highly positive words about Duvall's career to date: "To anyone who has been following his career, the star turn is Robert Duvall as the German staff officer who plans the operation. . . . His last films were *The Seven-Per-Cent Solution,* in which he played Holmes's Dr. Watson with a flawless English public-school accent, and *Network,* in which he was a high-level hustler. Here, well made-up with subtle bone structure, he is a stiff clever colonel with eye patch and one black glove."

Following this Erich von Stroheim-style German-general performance, Duvall had to switch back to crazy Kilgore. There were still a few more scenes to shoot, but the typhoons had wreaked havoc with the schedule. So it was back to the Philippines for a few more weeks, with a stopover in Malibu to reacquire the necessary tan. Then, a year and a half later, television gave him another military role that was the antithesis of Kilgore—that of Dwight David Eisenhower.

Duvall was very pleased to be offered the leading role in "Ike: The War Years." Not only was the money good and the exposure extensive, but also he genuinely admired the general. It was a role close to the heart of the man who was once a boy at the Annapolis naval base waiting for his father to come home from the fighting in the North Atlantic.

Duvall saw Ike as "the personification of good," and Hitler as "the personification of evil." Ike, Duvall explains, "was in the right place at the right time in history. The European war theater was black and white. It was the good guys against the bad guys. And Ike, being of German descent, was ashamed of the Nazis. It was his personal mission to do away with them. During this part of his life I admired him immensely."

The heat of this admiration sent some sparks flying between Duvall and the drama's author and producer, Melville Shavelson. There were quarrels about the script and a whopping personality clash, but underlying both was probably the possessiveness actor and author each felt about "his" Ike. Shavelson was directing the United States and North African sequences in Los Angeles, after which the English portion would be filmed in London and the surrounding countryside under the direction of Boris Sagal.

Enraged over the conflicts with Shavelson, Duvall, as the press put it, "took a hike from the Ike set." He walked away from the Los Angeles set in April 1978 and flew back to New York immediately. Five days later he was back in California, ready to go to work. The producer had conceded to Duvall's demands for script changes. It wasn't that Shavelson had to have Duvall at that point; it was simply too expensive to look around for another Ike now that the shooting was under way.

The Duvall who stormed off the "Ike" set was the same actor who had threatened to take Henry Hathaway to the union. Only now he had reached the point in his movie career where he was working exclusively with directors with whom he had an affinity. He hadn't taken such precautions with this miniseries and so found himself clashing with a director at a time in his life when he felt he should be past such hassles. There was no way he was going to work with a script with which he wasn't satisfied when he was portraying someone he deeply admired.

The production proceeded peacefully after such a turbulent beginning. Duvall was working with some excellent actors—Dana Andrews, who played General George Marshall; Darren McGavin, who was cast as General George S. Patton; and Lee Remick, with whom he had worked so well in *Wait Until Dark* on Broadway a dozen years earlier.

Lee Remick's role caused even more controversy than Duvall's Ike had. She was playing Kay Summersby, the spunky Englishwoman who was Eisenhower's driver through blitz-scarred London and whose memoirs were an important source for the script. The Eisenhower family was indignant upon hearing how prominent a role Summersby had in the drama and withdrew all their support from the project. The love story is sufficiently toned down so that there's no overt affair, but Duvall and Remick give very good performances as two people intensely attracted to each other. In fact, the almost-love story overshadows any other aspect of the series.

When the six-million-dollar project was aired on ABC in March 1979, it received a lot of attention and primarily favorable reviews. The critics were impressed with the photography: how black-and-white newsreel footage was converted via a "colorization" computer-controlled process to match the rest of the film. While they thought Lee Remick did a fine job with the Summersby role, they felt that her prominence in the drama gave it a soap-opera quality.

The reception to Duvall's Eisenhower was quite favorable. The consensus was that the actor had interpreted the general just right—as a simple man from Kansas dealing with a superhuman responsibility; as a man who was as quick to anger as he was to sympathize; as a man who was essentially very decent, handling overwhelming pressures with spirit and dignity.

Half a year after the public watched Duvall portray the best of the military as Ike on TV, they saw his performance of its flip side in the lunacy of Kilgore. *Apocalypse Now* finally opened in New York in August 1979. Anticipation of the event was sky-high thanks to the production's media appeal. Stories about the swollen budget, the series of calamities, and the colorful excesses on the set were grabbed up by the press.

That Coppola was going to extremes was obvious to anyone who was following the drama in the Philippines, but it was brought home to him by his wife, Eleanor, who expressed her concern about his excessive expenditures and impetuous gestures in a telex she sent to him on the set, with copies going to key people in the production. This well-meaning but scarcely welcome missive was intended to make her husband realize that "he was setting up his own Vietnam with his supply lines of wine and steaks and air conditioners. Creating the very conditions he went there to expose. That with his staff of hundreds of people carrying out his every request he was turning into Kurtz—going too far."

With the Philippines chapter of his moviemaking ordeal completed, Coppola was back home in San Francisco, facing the most difficult task of all—cutting and editing a film out of the massive footage he had shot. Unfortunately, one of the scenes he chose to eliminate was one of Duvall's. In it, Kilgore saves the life of a Vietnamese child and then goes back to talking about surfing. This omission badly hurt Duvall because he felt that showing Kilgore for a moment in a sympathetic light brought out the contradictions in the man. He always wanted to go for the complexity in a character, but had to withstand the tendency of moviemakers to oversimplify and stereotype. In the same way that Brando wouldn't let an unsympathetic side to Don Corleone be shown, so Coppola was willing to sacrifice a glimpse of another, more appealing side to Kilgore.

That cut scene rankled as much as those omitted from *Tomorrow* had hurt. "It happens in every film I'm in," Duvall complained. "There's a scene cut, and it's always a scene where I've put in a little brush stroke."

But even without the brush stroke, it was Duvall's performance that received the most emphatic acclaim amid the mixed reviews *Apocalypse Now* accumulated. Coppola had anticipated the nature of the criticisms his opus would evoke when he had taken an unfinished version to the Cannes Film Festival a few months earlier, when he was still undecided about which of several alternative endings he would use. In talking about the film in Cannes, Coppola admitted: "We made it the way Americans made war in Vietnam. There were too many of us, too much money and equipment, and little by little we went insane. I thought I was making a war film and it developed that the film was making me. The jungle was making a film."

When the picture opened in New York the critics concurred with this painfully frank self-evaluation. "A stunning work—as technically complex and masterful as any war film I can remember . . . an adventure yarn with delusions of grandeur" was how Vincent Canby put it. In his *New West* review, Stephen Farber said that the movie "unwittingly mirrors the spirit of the Vietnam War. . . . A hollow exercise in logistics, an oversized catastrophe." The general consensus was that *Apocalypse Now* was visually spectacular but lacked an emotional context, that the parallels with Conrad didn't work, and that the characters' motivations and moral dilemmas were never clarified.

Except for Kilgore. Everyone understood Kilgore and had nothing but praise for the actor who portrayed the only character to successfully convey Coppola's theme. *Newsweek*'s Jack Kroll wrote that Kilgore's attack on the Viet Cong-held beach was "extraordinary in its complexity and savage vertiginous energy . . . the episode combines a fearsome violence with the surrealistic madness of Kilgore, brilliantly played by Robert Duvall. . . ."

"Kilgore's surrealistic excesses are generated not by the demands of comedy but by demands from inside a realistic character. Kilgore is a mutant" was Veronica Geng's astute comment in *The New Yorker*.

When Duvall was staying in New York's Plaza Hotel for the late-summer opening of the war epic, the press tried to get him to make his contribution to the media hype surrounding the event. "It's a great film," he simply told them, "and Coppola is the director I like working with best but the film to me means a job three years ago. It's *his* obsession."

Their professional paths haven't crossed since, although they have remained friends. Coppola has made movies since *Apocalypse Now,* but none has generated the interest of that picture or *The Godfather* epic preceding it. It's as though the jungle burned something out of Hollywood's raging young genius, aging him and, perhaps, sapping some of his creative juices. Duvall's career took another direction; leading roles in far more modest productions rather than supporting parts in lavish ones.

Kilgore on that beach extolling the virtues of morning napalm remains one of Duvall's screen triumphs. His skepticism with Coppola's obsessions was always there. Just as he had commented that real hoods had a viciousness *The Godfather*'s screen ones lacked, so he made the point that "nobody who's been in a war movie in the last five years has actually been in a war."

He could brilliantly show the mad fanaticism of a Kilgore, but he deeply resented that an episode revealing another dimension to the character was omitted from the film's final version. Nevertheless, Kilgore represents Duvall at his best, in a role demanding all the flamboyance he had had to hold in check in so many earlier roles. This actor, with his unique skill at capturing just the right nuances for inarticulate Southerners and for desperadoes on both sides of the law, was displaying a rare sensitivity in portraying men at war.

Bull Meechum is a man who would love to be at war, only there isn't any—not in America in 1962—so Bull turns his home into a boot camp. Bull is Kilgore in peacetime, according to critics who noted the continuity between the two parts, both men being fanatical fliers. If the two characters are similar, their movies are direct opposites. *Apocalypse Now* was made with more fanfare than just about any motion picture in history—and turned out to be a disappointment in many respects. *The Great Santini* was made with no frills, was almost buried alive, and was then saved at the eleventh hour to win its fair share of critical accolades.

The Great Santini's voyage from obscurity to acclaim could be a movie in itself—maybe an exposé-style treatment of the way pictures are financed, produced, and marketed in an industry geared to the blockbuster; or perhaps a perils-of-Pauline-type tale of a daring rescue just in the nick of time. All the ingredients are there, be it exposé or melodrama.

The Great Santini started out as a novel by Pat Conroy, an unabashedly autobiographical story of a sensitive boy growing up and into conflict with his father, a swaggering Marine Corps officer. When the author's father first read his son's book, he furiously threw it away without finishing it; then he retrieved it and read on, through tears of self-recognition, to the end.

Now an enterprising producer, Charles A. Pratt, enters the scene. The head of Bing Crosby Productions, Pratt buys the screen rights to Conroy's novel in September 1977. A World War II vet, Pratt feels such an affinity for the book that he decides to produce the picture himself. He finds an award-winning New York City playwright, Lewis John Carlino, who believes as strongly in the story as he does, and they're off.

Carlino writes a script that Pratt submits to United Artists, which contracts to buy half the film's $4 million budget.

Now the plot thickens. The senior executives at United Artists rise up and resign en masse and launch Orion Pictures, but in their hasty departure they leave *The Great Santini* behind to be shuffled aside by their harried successors. His United Artists deal canceled, Pratt takes his project to the newly formed Orion outfit, and a new deal is made.

Pratt sends the script to several actors, among them Bobby Duvall. Of course he loves it. What could be closer to him than a story about a boy growing up in a military family? And Lieutenant Colonel Meechum is as crazy as Lieutenant Colonel Kilgore, but he's a lot of other things, too. Finally, a character with the contradictions that make for dramatic conflict, with complexity enough to challenge any actor instead of the simplicity of a two-dimensional stereotype. It's also the lead. Robert Duvall wants the Meechum part as badly as he's wanted any role—and he gets it.

The rest of the casting is done around Duvall; Pratt and Carlino search around New York and come up with Blythe Danner and Michael O'Keefe for the wife and son. With the casting complete and Carlino slated as director, they're ready for production. But they need technical assistance from the Marine Corps, which isn't too happy with the script, concerned that it might show the USMC in an unfavorable light.

Pat Conroy's aid is enlisted to attain the Corps's support. He writes a letter to the Marine Corps's public relations people, stressing the script's positive image of the Corps: "The leatherneck aviator lives life at high acceleration—on the cutting edge. He is a man of action, not of introspection. He is a warrior never quite comfortable in the milieu of his own home. He is motivated by the powerful mythology of the Marine aviator." Conroy's well-turned phrases convince the Marine Corps that *Santini* means them no harm and they offer technical assistance, provided a few negative images are deleted from the script. The necessary adjustments made, the technical assistance granted, the film goes into production at the Marine air station in Beaufort, South Carolina, where Pat Conroy was raised. Shooting starts in October 1978 and is completed by Christmas; by the following fall the lengthy cutting, editing, and scoring processes are finished. So far, so good. Now the scenario takes some odd turns.

November 1979: *The Great Santini is premiered in Beaufort, complete with a Marine band and color guard; there are simultaneous openings thoughout the Carolinas. Local reviews give the film high praise, but the box office receipts are low. The producers, the Orion people, who released the film, and their Warner Brothers distributors fret that the fault lies in the name, more appropriate to an Italian juggling act than to an emotional drama about a military family. They decide to test different titles in two-day engagements in small midwestern cities.*

January 1980: *In Fort Wayne, Indiana, the film opens as* Sons and Heroes; *in Rockford, Illinois, it's known as* Reaching Out, *and it plays in Peoria as* The Ace. *Although it does poorly in Peoria, it does twice as well there as in the other two cities, so* The Ace *it is.*

Spring 1980: The Ace *bombs in Cincinnati, Ohio, and in San Diego, Sacramento, Stockton, and Modesto. Pratt hangs in there; he's gone through this before when another Crosby Productions movie,* Walking Tall, *grossed $6 on its opening day in Lubbock, Texas. He urges Orion to try another approach: an exclusive New York engagement at a small theater to drum up word-of-mouth support for the picture.*

July 1980: *Pratt books* Santini *at a select movie house in Manhattan, only to find that Orion has sold the picture to Home Box Office and In-Flight motion pictures. He's enraged, but they tell him it's their only chance to salvage their investment. Pratt* *scrapes together enough money for an opening at the tiny Guild Theater under the movie's original title. A week later* The Great Santini *has garnered some rave reviews and grossed $40,000, an all-time record for the Guild. It's also being shown to 50,000 HBO subscribers in downtown Manhattan as* The Ace.

August 1980: Santini *opens at the Paris Cinema in Boston's elegant Back Bay, and is declared the best American movie of the year by* The Boston Globe's *critic Bruce McCabe, who's astonished to see such a gem turn up in the dog-day doldrums usually reserved for the grade-B material.* The Ace *is available for viewing by Washington, D.C.'s 23,000-household HBO subscribers.* The Great Santini *opens in a theater in Los Angeles and one in Philadelphia to glowing reviews.*

September 1980: The Great Santini *opens in the capital and is praised to the skies by* The Washington Post.

And that's the story of how movie buffs got to see *The Great Santini* in art theaters while HBO subscribers watched *The Ace* in their living rooms. The general conclusion to be drawn from this real-life drama is that if a movie's plot is not quickly classifiable, if it stars names like Duvall and Danner that aren't an instant box office draw—not to mention being burdened with an awkward title—its distributors can't hope to sell it through hinterland openings. But before they condemn it to the cable-TV and airline circuits, they should make every effort to have it reviewed by the most influential critics in cities with a serious cinema audience.

Rex Reed was impressed enough to write in New York's *Daily News* that *The Great Santini* has "not a false note, not a wrong move in it as it achieves a beautiful, lyrical balance between feelings and hard-edged reality. No element ever reaches the dangerous perimeter of cliché."

The praise was far from universal, with most of the criticism centering on the plot, which many found too fuzzy and too cluttered with extraneous themes like race relations in the South. The most positive viewpoints were expressed about the quality of the acting, particularly that of the lead. Duvall gives a fully fleshed portrait of a truly obnoxious man, but succeeds in eliciting the audience's empathy for the brute by making him so *comprehensible*. We feel his pain while abhorring his behavior. It's such an involving film that we experience him as the different members of his family do. We feel the mixture of nervous compassion and fond exasperation Blythe Danner's Lillian exhibits whenever he's around; the caring resentment Michael O'Keefe's Ben shows as the boy struggles to understand the restless competitive spirit driving his father; and the ridicule his feisty comic of a daughter is driven to heap upon him.

Vincent Canby best describes how the depth and subtlety of the characters lift the film above its limitations: "*The Great Santini* is not a great film. It has lapses of tone and style that would have wrecked better films. Yet it contains three beautifully realized characters and it risks unintentional laughter by probing these three characters to a depth not dared by most films."

Canby also took this opportunity in his *New York Times* review to make a significant observation on the power of Duvall's performance: "Perhaps never before in the history of American movies have there been so many first-rate leading actors doing so many different kinds of roles. I'm thinking specifically of Dustin Hoffman, Al Pacino, Robert Redford, Jack Nicholson, Clint Eastwood, Roy Scheider, Jon Voight, and, the most consistently surprising and rewarding of the lot, Robert Duvall. . . . Now it's about time to recognize Robert Duvall as one of the most resourceful, most technically proficient, most remarkable actors in America today. . . . At this moment, having just seen Mr. Duvall in *The*

Great Santini, I think he may well be the best we have, the American Olivier."

How typical of the maverick nature of Duvall's career that he should have gleaned such heady praise from so illustrious a source for his performance in a picture which was at that moment an HBO property. *The Great Santini* was in a sense Duvall's second leading role, the first significant one being *Tomorrow.* Actually, the first was *THX 1138,* but in an overall perspective his portrayal of someone with only a rudimentary personality could hardly be called pivotal. Sandwiched between *The Godfather* movies Duvall had made *Badge 373* and *The Outfit,* those back-to-back cops-and-robbers leads, but he always thought of them as character roles, and neither film gave him sufficient range to display his talent.

Tomorrow was, of course, a turning point for Duvall but remained obscure to the general public. *The Great Santini,* then, was Duvall's first lead that attracted the notice of the public as well as the critics. *Santini* had the basis for a broader popular appeal than *Tomorrow,* the distribution problems of both pictures aside. A movie about lively and sensitive adolescents coping with a belligerent, colorful father tugs at universal emotions that run strong and deep. More than a portrait of a heavy-drinking, brawling, outrageously competitive, superpatriotic marine flier, *Santini* is the story of a family and has in it elements common to all families, thereby evoking recognition in anyone who has ever been locked in conflict with a parent.

Did Duvall strongly identify with the Michael O'Keefe role when he was making the movie? Of course, the circumstances were reminiscent of his youth—the military base, the mother full of warmth and charm running the household on a more lenient basis during her officer husband's absence, an impressionable boy who has yet to find where he belongs in the world confronting a father whose identity lies in his commitment to his military career. But there the similarity ends, despite simplistic attempts to draw a more direct parallel between the lieutenant colonel and the rear admiral. A few years later when his Oscar piqued public curiosity about the actor's background, some glib journalistic comparisons were made between the biographical facts of Duvall's life and the *Santini* role. It's easy enough to dispel such facile analogies by trying to imagine Bull Meechum urging Ben to study acting, as William Duvall did with Bodge. The image boggles the mind.

The perfection of Duvall's performance elicits such attempts to pigeonhole his sources. He's so thoroughly the part he's playing that it's easy to imagine this is Robert Duvall's adolescence we're seeing in Ben Meechum; but it's Pat Conroy's. It's Conroy's father Duvall is playing, or rather, his interpretation of Conroy's portrait of the blustering Marine in whose shadow he was raised. In Conroy's novel, Bull Meechum was a swaggering six feet four inches; for Duvall it was Eddie Carbone again, or Boo Radley, acting his way to resembling a large man despite his average stature and slight build. His Meechum *is* big, with his thick, booming voice and boisterous gestures. He dominates everyone around him with the flamboyance of his antics and the absurdity of his attitudes.

There's an exuberance about the brash Meechum that Kilgore had in abundance. But Kilgore got just a few scenes in which to do his strutting, and the one that gave a brief glimpse of another aspect of him was cut, while Meechum has a whole movie in which to flex his muscles and rave and rant. Getting the chance to flaunt that exuberance, to demonstrate that energy, was a great relief to Duvall after the

more restrained performances previous scripts had demanded of him.

Frank Burns in *M*A*S*H* is as contemptible in his way as
Bull is in his; the ruthless TV executive's actions in *Network*
are as menacing as Meechum's in his tantrums and tirades.
But those earlier roles called for what Pauline Kael termed
Duvall's "genius" for "keeping himself in the background."
His Meechum is flagrantly in the foreground, and Duvall
relished the chance to show what he could do there, though
his dramatic feats were very nearly lost to all but HBO subscribers and passengers on particular air flights.

Duvall's role in *The Great Santini* is nobody's idea of a sympathetic character, and Duvall doesn't go for the easy touch
of sentimentality to soften his contours. He's an SOB if ever
there was one. Nor is he anybody's idea of a stock villain.
This is a man who's truly in love with his wife, as well as
being emotionally dependent on her emotional support.
He's a man who cares fiercely for his children, but he's also
an overbearing egomaniac who can't stop competing with
his son, taunting him mercilessly after the boy beats him in
a basketball contest.

The more glaring the contradictions, the more challenging the role, has always been the way Duvall looks at a part.
He plays Meechum like a jigsaw puzzle of disparate parts
that fit together to form one highly complex and miserable
human being. This is no trite variation on the tough-on-the-
outside, tender-on-the-inside routine. Bull Meechum's a
bully, all right, and there are components in his personality
that are downright despicable. He's also a frightened, vulnerable man, alienated from the family he so confusedly
loves, fast becoming a misfit in the Marine Corps he so desperately needs. And it's that character, rife with ambiguities
and contradictions, that Duvall brings to the screen. Creat-

ing a whole person who evokes both contempt and compassion is a kind of dramatic juggling act; so, maybe *The Great Santini* isn't an inappropriate title after all.

Despite the sense of human complexity with which Duvall tackled the Bull Meechum role, there were critics who reacted to it with their own brand of stereotypic thinking, such as Veronica Geng, who wrote in *The SoHo Weekly News* that *The Great Santini* tries "to provide an environment of justification and understanding for a military man much like the one Robert Duvall played in *Apocalypse Now*."

Although there's a lot of surface similarity in the two roles, the continuity between them can be drawn too far. Kilgore symbolizes a war insane in its pointless destruction. Meechum's story has a timeless quality to it: he's any man who knows more about fighting than about loving, who's at home in a war, out of his element in peacetime. But *The Great Santini* is more a family drama than a study of a military mentality. Bull Meechum could be just as macho and intractable in another walk of life, and the movie's basic ingredient of familial conflict would still be there. But Kilgore could be only on that Vietnamese beachhead with his chopper and surfboard; there's no other time or place in which his existence would be possible.

Duvall was interested in playing challenging roles rather than in stereotyping military men. Between Kilgore and Bull Meechum, he played Eisenhower. Probably one of the reasons for his fury over the problems with the "Ike" miniseries script is that for once he could play the soldier as hero, and he didn't want that tampered with.

The Kilgore role won Duvall an Oscar nomination for Best Supporting Actor and *Santini* a nomination for Best Actor. In both parts he had tried to show the contradictions in the man, but the scene that added another dimension to Kilgore was considered expendable by Coppola in the cutting room. Even with *Santini*, where the characterization was multilayered, there was a scene cut that focused on a softer side of the macho protagonist. Duvall was disappointed that the scene in which Meechum presents his daughter with flowers for her first formal dance wasn't included in the final version of the film.

Personally, he always saw a lot more to admire than to disparage in military men. Some people become artists to live a different life from their parents; Bobby lived a different life from William and Mildred Duvall *because* he was an artist. His values never strayed far from theirs. Given the difference in generations and the fact that his life is lived in the fast-paced entertainment world, Robert Duvall's attitudes are quite similar to his family's.

Duvall is a man who prefers the simple and the direct when it comes to expressing thoughts and feelings. He has a healthy sense of skepticism when it comes to elaborate theories and messages. He could admire Coppola's artistry and like the man personally, but still keep a distance from those grandiose concepts with which the director was always toying. He could admire Vanessa Redgrave's acting but have no patience for her Trotskyite politics, chuckling over the fact that the cameramen on the set of *The Seven-Per-Cent Solution* would duck when they saw her coming, spouting her leftist dogmas. Duvall has never had any patience with hypocrisy and has no respect for the kind of wealthy liberals who argue for busing but send their children to private schools. Yet he doesn't discuss these issues often, maintaining that political beliefs, like religious ones, are private matters.

One of the reasons why Duvall was so effective in *The Great Santini* was that he wasn't satirizing a type but portraying an individual. Yet just being on the set of a military base had to evoke some childhood memories in him. The two months he spent in Beaufort, South Carolina, making the film were a welcome respite from the pressures of New York. He rented a lovely house on a creek and savored the tranquility.

It was nearly Christmas by the time they were through shooting that emotionally involving story of a military family. Old ties were tugging strongly on Bobby. He'd been going through a difficult time. His personal life was in chaos, and his professional one was increasingly absorbed with a project he lacked the funds to complete. He needed to get away for a while; he needed to go home. He went back to Alexandria, where, after the holidays, he rented an old house near where his parents lived. He spent his time raising money for his project, munching on his mother's Maryland crab cakes and making music with his brothers. And he spent time with the reassuring figure of his father, the retired rear admiral, the military man of Bodge's earliest memories, who was such a far cry from those macho fighting machines Bobby Duvall portrayed so brilliantly on the screen.

Duvall made his movie debut in 1963 as the shy recluse Boo Radley in *To Kill a Mockingbird*.

In *Captain Newman, M.D.* Duvall played a young officer recovering from a nervous breakdown under the care of psychiatrist Gregory Peck and nurse Angie Dickinson.

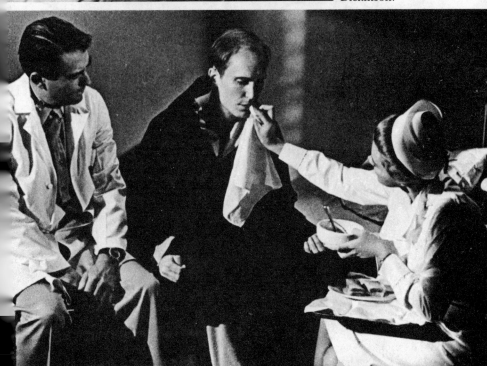

As a cab driver
taxiing Steve
McQueen around
San Francisco in
Bullitt, Duvall made
the most of a bit part.

Portraying the first of
many movie-villain
roles, Duvall played
the bad guy in John
Wayne's masterpiece,
True Grit.

Burt Lancaster had the title role and Duvall was the outlaw in *Lawman*.

It's high-comedy time in *M*A*S*H* when Duvall as Frank Burns and Sally Kellerman as Major Hot Lips hop into bed.

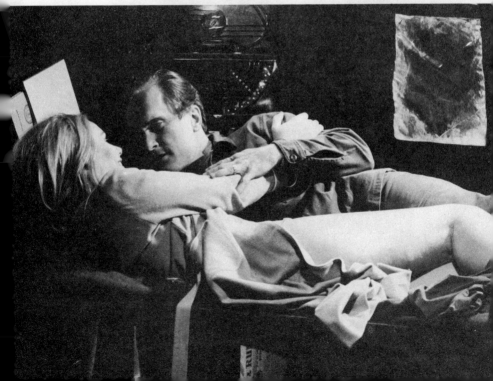

With Shirley
Knight as a
troubled
housewife who's
hit the road,
Duvall played a
tough cop with a
tender side in *The
Rain People*.

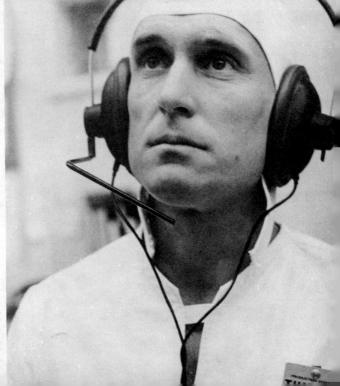

His first movie
lead was in the
title role of *THX
1138*, a futuristic
adventure story
filmed in 1970.

Duvall in his favorite role as the haggard and tragic dirt farmer, Jackson Fentry, in Horton Foote's adaptation of William Faulkner's *Tomorrow*.

As the trusted *consiglieri* Tom Hagen, Duvall proffered advice to Michael Corleone in *The Godfather, Part II*.

(Above) With his first wife, Barbara Benjamin, Duvall attended a pre-Academy Awards party in 1973.

(Below) Robert Duvall and Faye Dunaway as a pair of ruthless TV executives in the savage and farcical satire, *Network*.

Between his two marriages Duvall hung out a lot with actor Paul Gleason, a star of the daytime serial *All My Children*.

Duvall donned British duds and assumed an Oxford accent to play the ever-loyal Dr. Watson in a new look at the Sherlock Holmes legend, *The Seven-Per-Cent Solution*.

Made up to the hilt, Duvall effectively portrayed a German officer in the World War II thriller, *The Eagle Has Landed.*

In the 1978 TV miniseries, *Ike: The War Years,* Duvall and Lee Remick were convincing as General Eisenhower and his British companion, Kay Summersby.

Duvall's crazed Lt. Colonel Kilgore stole the show in Francis Coppola's Vietnam War epic, *Apocalypse Now*.

(Above) As the brash, brawling Marine air ace, Bull Meechum, in *The Great Santini,* Duvall blazed with maniacal energy.

(Below) In *The Betsy,* featuring Jane Alexander, Duvall played the scion of an automotive dynasty.

(Above) In *True Confessions* Duvall and De Niro gave intense performances as the Spellacy brothers, a hardboiled detective and an ambitious priest.

(Below) Robert Duvall, John Savage, and Kenneth McMillan as a trio of small-time hoods in David Mamet's Broadway play, *American Buffalo*.

The actor discovers a new talent in Angelo Evans and decides to make a movie about the beguiling, street-smart gypsy boy.

The director-producer-scriptwriter, and his star—Duvall and Evans on the set of *Angelo, My Love.*

(Above) Duvall succeeded in capturing the squalor and exotica of New York's gypsy community in scenes such as this depiction of a ritual trial.

(Below) With Eric Fryer as the valiant young Canadian cancer victim, Duvall played a supporting role in HBO's *The Terry Fox Story*.

In *The Natural*, starring Robert Redford, Duvall played Max Mercy, a shrewd sportswriter.

A year after their 1982 marriage, Bobby and Gail Duvall show smiles of happiness to the press.

With Tess Harper as his young wife and Allan Hubbard as his stepson, Duvall played the washed-up country and western singer, Mac Sledge, in *Tender Mercies*.

(*Above*) Inspired by his new family, Mac Sledge returns to the stage, an important step in rebuilding his life.

(*Below*) Duvall's moment of triumph arrives when he wins an Oscar as Best Actor for his portrayal of Mac Sledge in *Tender Mercies*.

7

RAGE OF A GUTTER RAT

The painful chaos in Duvall's personal life was brought
about by his separation from Barbara in 1975. Their marriage had lasted ten years, and in that time he'd made a lot
of movies. Following *The Godfather* films, he had begun to
savor the sweet taste of success. He'd spent a lot of time in
Hollywood and on location, but always there was the bedrock of his home to return to, the sprawling old house in
the serene suburb, the children and the animals, the delights of riding his own horses and playing on his own tennis court. The marriage had given him the feeling of
emotional security and the stability of fatherhood. But it
didn't hold up for the long haul.

The habitual restlessness that motivated Duvall to seek
such a wide variety of roles and formed his preference for
short-run theater engagements may have made him discon-
tented with the leveling off a marriage undergoes after a
decade. He needed that edge of excitement the marriage
could no longer provide; he once compared a long marriage to doing a play too many nights. Although he is very
much the devoted family man, Duvall also has something of
the loner about him. Traveling so much, he got to enjoy
being on his own. It was no longer the same with Barbara,
and the restlessness was getting to him, making him increasingly dissatisfied at home. A movie actor is always attractive to women, even if he doesn't fit the star image. A

wife whose life is centered on home and family can greatly resent her husband's absences, especially when her children are growing up and are less dependent on her. The tension between the Duvalls grew, and they decided to separate.

On his own, Bobby very soon moved in with an airline stewardess in her late twenties who had an apartment in Queens. She had a childlike quality he found beguiling, and she traveled with him to far-flung locations whenever possible. He was constantly on the go for his career, which was blossoming even as his marital life was fading. He was in San Francisco filming *The Killer Elite;* in New York to make *Network;* in England for *The Seven-Per-Cent Solution;* in the Philippines for *Apocalypse Now;* and back to England for *The Eagle Has Landed,* even managing to squeeze in a role as a sleazy fight promotor in Muhammed Ali's *The Greatest,* filmed in Florida.

On the tail end of that hectic period, Bobby and Barbara faced the fact that reconciliation wasn't possible and decided to get a divorce. That difficult decision made, there was the usual eruption of monetary disputes. He was the one making the money; she was the one who felt like the aggrieved party. Those kinds of contentions can get ugly, and the affection still existing between the two was overwhelmed by the financial hassles.

At the same time, Bobby was undergoing another kind of divorce. He had decided not to marry the woman with whom he had been living for the last year and a half. Much as he cared for her, he didn't want to go from one marriage to another; he didn't feel ready to settle down again. The bitterness between him and Barbara was hurting Duvall, and he knew he never wanted to go through another divorce proceeding. He needed to be on his own awhile. Although certain he'd made the right decision, Duvall went through a bad time. It was like getting *two* divorces, one from the woman he'd loved enough to marry, and another from one with whom he was in love but not ready to marry. In an interview with Lindsy Van Gelder during this unsettling period, he was uncustomarily frank about his personal life. When the *New York Post* columnist asked him if the two women in his life were alike, his reply was, "Yeah, Jewish. I said to Jimmy Caan once, 'What is it with me and Jewish women?' He said, 'They see the husband in you, Bobby.'"

That husband in him got obscured for a while, but it was still there, buried under the surface of a man in a hesitant mood about commitments. Caan, who was famous for his macho charm and exuberant womanizing, was aware of the matrimonial propensity in his intense friend. Caan recalls Duvall urging him to "fix him up" with a woman: "So I brought this dynamite girl over to his hotel room, and he acted as gross as possible to turn her off, and she left. He was really relieved. He's a more traditional guy. You watch, he'll get married and be better off for it."

Duvall *was* more traditional than a lot of his friends and had never been a womanizer. Women had always found Bobby attractive, and he them, but it was relationships he cared about, not conquests. That's why he liked to focus his energies on one woman at a time. When he was living alone and without a steady girl friend he would go out, but it wasn't a comfortable situation for him. He missed the security of marriage, even while he feared its restraints.

"I'm just trying to get it together in a quiet way," he told Lindsy Van Gelder in that candid interview. "I don't know where it's going or anything. I still miss my wife. They say you never get over your first mate, and we were always good friends up until the end. We had the same interests. And I like somebody putting that food in front of me while I'm watching the Super Bowl."

But that domestic coziness wasn't in the cards for him—at

least not yet. The decision to make the separation from Barbara permanent with a divorce and the breakup with his live-in lover doubled his loneliness and emotional confusion.

It was as though he were reliving his earlier bachelor days when Duvall, in January 1977, returned to live full-time in Manhattan, something he hadn't done since he left the city fifteen years before. That had been in 1962 when, after his run in *The Days and Nights of Beebee Fenstermaker*, he'd moved out to California, only to return a year and a half later with a wife and two children and settle down in Tuxedo Park. In some ways it was the old days all over again, but in others it was different. He was back on the Upper West Side, in a small brownstone apartment, but now he was living alone while then there had been a stream of roommates in and out and a group of kindred spirits—other struggling young actors—to hang out with. Now most of the old gang were married, for the second if not the first time, and spread out across the country. But Bobby still had a lot of friends, because with his gregarious nature he had never stopped making them.

He was the informal "coach" of "Adult Day Camp," a mobile coterie of friends and acquaintances who got together on whatever coast they found themselves to play tennis and touch football, go body surfing and horseback riding, and get together for singing and guitar strumming. There was Day Camp East for whomever of that mobile bunch happened to be working or playing in the Big Apple at the time, and there was Day Camp West for those who were out on the Coast. Of course, the sun and surf were much easier to come by in California, where Duvall would rent a house in Malibu for his stays there. Friends like Jimmy Caan, Kris Kristoffersen, Burt Young, Wayne Rogers, Duvall's agent, Merritt Blake, and the character actor Harry Dean Stanton would come around to swim and surf and sing.

Duvall always relished this male camaraderie, the horsing around, the shared zest for sports. Athletics remained very important to Duvall, and in his mid-forties in the mid-1970s, his strenuous workouts plus the absence of alcohol, tobacco, and even coffee from his routine kept him in excellent shape, well able to hold his own in competition with men considerably younger than himself. In 1975 he entered television's "Superstar Decathlon" for actor-athletes, jauntily wearing a hat labeled "Old Man of the Mountain." The "old man" won in ten grueling events against actors half his age.

Duvall always surrounds himself with a variety of people, never having lost his youthful thirst for studying a broad range of humanity. But his friends are not just sources for studying traits he can file away for future roles, memories to which he can refer for characterizations. They are companions with whom he likes to hang out, play tennis and softball, go on fishing and canoe trips. One of his favorite pals during the time he was married to Barbara was a redneck he'd met in North Carolina named Danny Greenway, whose country expressions always appealed to Duvall. Once when Bobby went to pick up Barbara at the airport, he took Danny Greenway along. "Honey, Bobby's been waiting for you. He wants to do a few U-turns under the sheets" was the greeting Mrs. Duvall received.

After the breakup of his marriage, his friends and their activities became increasingly important to Duvall as a buffer against the loneliness a separation carries in its wake. At Malibu there was not only Adult Day Camp West, but a night version of the daytime activities where things could get pretty rowdy. A journalist who once spent some time with Duvall and his pal Paul Gleason, the actor and former baseball player, heard Gleason say to Duvall: "Remember when I was with that Polish gymnast—boy, was she dumb, but what a body—and you came in with nothing but your hat on?"

From hints like that, it's easy to imagine the revelries on those moonlit Mailbu nights when Day Camp sun and fun turned to nocturnal romps and games. Gleason had a gutsy kind of recklessness Bobby enjoyed. He went with Duvall to Miami in 1976, where the actor was getting $50,000 for two days' shooting in Muhammad Ali's *The Greatest*. They stayed at the Palm Bay Club for the tennis. Duvall, who has played in Pro-Am tennis matches in Arizona and Florida, was taking his game as seriously as ever. When Duvall met Ali, the Champ told him he wanted to get into acting and that he had seen Duvall in a lot of Westerns. Duvall and Gleason then did an improvisation of a Western to show Ali what was involved. Bobby quickly cast the fighter as a stranger in town and Gleason as the sheriff who's chasing him out of town.

"We don't want you in this town," Gleason told Ali in a sheriff's rough tone.

"What if I don't want to leave?" Ali asked. "You ain't big enough to make me."

Gleason was really getting into his role. "Hey, man," he told the world's heavyweight champion, "get your black ass out!"

From the look in Ali's eye, Gleason thought he'd had it, but then the Champ took two steps back and put his huge hands where his guns would have been. "Draw," he said.

Duvall's friendships existed on many levels. With Greenway he relished the country humor; with Gleason and Caan the clowning around, the sports activities, and the occasional pursuit of lovely ladies. With Ulu Grosbard, he had a quieter sort of connection. They didn't see each other that often, but the lines of mutual respect and trust had been firmly established and they continued to hold each other in the highest professional esteem. That's why when Grosbard told Duvall he was doing a play by a young Chicago playwright and he wanted Bobby to have the lead, Duvall read the script with great interest.

Any play Ulu sent would have to be good because the idealistic director would deal only with that which had true artistic merit. At forty-eight, Grosbard had painstakingly acquired the reputation of a perfectionist who would not go into production unless he was working with a finely polished script and the best possible cast. When asked if it were possible to maintain these high standards, his answer was, "Only if you're willing to pay the price—which is not working." This willingness to sacrifice work for artistic standards was the reason why a director so widely admired on both coasts had only seven professional productions in New York and two movies under his directorial belt.

But that was the way Ulu Grosbard wanted it. He and Rose Gregorio, his wife of a dozen years, had stuck by the promises they had made to themselves and each other back in the exuberant *Beebee Fenstermaker* days and nights—to participate only in those projects they found worthy of their talents. They happily shared a modest Bohemian life-style in their Greenwich Village apartment; and they still glowed with the fires of a creative sensibility that had never compromised its integrity.

One of Grosbard's biggest successes on Broadway was *The Subject Was Roses*. The producers of that play, Joseph Beruh and Edgar Lansbury, sent Grosbard the script of a play called *American Buffalo* by David Mamet. Grosbard was immediately interested. "I felt I was in the presence of an original voice in the American theater," Grosbard said, "with a unique vision, intelligence, an extraordinary ear for translating real behavior, who could capture in dialogue what is not being said, and who could do that with a class of people that is never represented in the American theater. I couldn't believe that he was twenty-eight and not from a lower-class background."

Instead, David Mamet came from a middle-class family in suburban Chicago. He went to Goddard College, a progressive school in Vermont where he studied drama, wanting to be an actor. But Mamet soon found that his theoretical ideas about acting were a long way from his ability to implement them. His colorful job history included teaching acting at Goddard and Marlboro colleges, and at Illinois Pontiac State Penitentiary; hustling Ping-Pong; playing poker; and being one of the founders of Chicago's St. Nicholas Theater Co., where his first plays were performed.

American Buffalo takes place in a cluttered Chicago junk shop where three scruffy characters are planning a robbery that never comes off. As soon as he read it, Grosbard knew that Duvall would be perfect as the lead, Teach, a tough, small-time thief and ex-con. So vividly did Grosbard see Bobby as Teach that in his first phone conversation with Mamet, the one demand he made was that, if Robert Duvall was available, the Teach part would be his. This condition posed no problem for the playwright, who was an avid Duvall fan.

Duvall liked the Teach part right away, finding the disreputable character wonderfully direct, lively, and colorful. He agreed to do the play, committing himself for a four-month engagement. Why, his lawyer and agent and the press asked him, when he would be paid only a fraction of what he made on a movie? There were several answers: He wanted to do a play again and hadn't done one since *Wait Until Dark* in 1966; he wanted to work with Ulu Grosbard again and hadn't since *A View from the Bridge* in 1965. He also thought the play could lead to some interesting movie parts; Teach was a character exuding energy, albeit a maniacal one, and in that pre-*Santini* period Duvall was playing parts calling for a practiced restraint. And he wanted a change from the grueling pace of moviemaking of the last few years, and from the emotional rigors of an impending divorce and the breakup of a relationship he valued. So it was back to Broadway early in 1977, moving into the bachelor apartment in January and starting rehearsals for the February opening at the Ethel Barrymore Theatre. The rehearsals were exciting because Grosbard was so skillful a director and the cast so perfectly matched. The beefy actor Kenneth McMillan played the aging fence who owned the junk shop; slim, young, and handsome John Savage played a dumb apprentice thug; and Duvall played the fast-talking, menacing Teach.

The part called for an enormous expenditure of energy, and Duvall gave it all he had, so much so that at the opening night performance when Teach is having a tantrum, throwing things around the junk shop, some pieces of tin went flying out into the orchestra.

He had played plenty of tough guys before, but Teach was the most volatile. Although he had already made *Apocalypse Now,* that film wouldn't be seen by the critics and the public for another two and a half years, so they had never seen Duvall with all the restraints off before. It made quite an impression.

Clive Barnes said in *The New York Times* that in a "complex and nervy" role, Duvall "alternates between self-pity and wild gusts of paranoid fury. His body is like a clenched fist, his manner has the danger of a rattlesnake, and he talks with a childlike tone of pure, sweet unreason."

"I have always admired Robert Duvall for the strength he gets from restraint; here, as a nervous burglar whose braggadocio outweighs his second-story skills, he fills the stage with a wacky, manic energy," commented Howard Kissel in *Women's Wear Daily,* while in *Time,* Christopher Porterfield said, "Duvall crackles with the quality Ingmar Bergman once said he looked for above all others in an actor: danger."

While the critics were lavishing their praises on Duvall's Teach, Duvall's friends were concerned that he was at that point in his career willing to act in a play for four months for about $50,000, half of what he'd made for the ten weeks of shooting *Network.* But he kept insisting that "doing a play makes you a better actor. . . . Getting into a play is like winning at Wimbledon. It may be less money than World Championship tennis, but it's more prestigious; you become the first, Number One—you're doing something that a lot of other actors can't do."

Duvall was as deeply immersed in Teach as he was in any character he ever played. Before the play opened, he'd flown down to Miami to see a guy he knew there, a teamster who'd been in prison, as had Teach. He talked to the man, observed his mannerisms, and picked up the trick of tucking his .38 revolver in a belt over his genitals because the cops wouldn't think of searching there. When he left Miami that ex-con's memories were with Duvall, and he took them onto the stage as Teach. He remained absolutely the hoodlum, even through a curtain call one night when there was no applause. He responded à la Teach by making an obscene gesture at the audience with his finger.

But people like Hoffman, Hackman, and Caan were still after Duvall about why he wasn't paying more attention to his career. When he went to lunch with Dustin Hoffman at a fashionable restaurant in the East Fifties, Duvall's old friend lectured him about how acting was a business, the actor an entrepreneur. But Duvall wasn't listening, just pretending to, as he thought about a trip he was planning up to

Ron Homberg's tennis camp in Kent, Connecticut. He was convinced he was good enough to beat Ron in a few games. As Duvall's thoughts followed a ball over a net, Hoffman gave him an exasperated nudge. "Bobby, you've got to start working on your career."

"F—— my career," Duvall countered. "I'm working on my forehand."

Ulu Grosbard was well aware of Duvall's carelessness about figuring out where his best interests lay. "Duvall is the least career-conscious actor I know," Grosbard said of the man he so deeply admired. "Al Pacino and Dustin Hoffman weigh all the career factors before they make a decision. Duvall is all actor; he looks at the part and doesn't worry about what it's going to do to his career. . . . He's the purest actor I know. By pure I mean in the way of a medieval craftsman. The craft means more to him than to any other actor I know. When I saw him twenty years ago in summer stock, I knew I was in the presence of a great actor. I saw the man transformed in front of my eyes. It was magic."

And Grosbard was seeing that same magic every night at the Ethel Barrymore Theatre as Duvall turned into the strident, shifty Teach. Well-intentioned friends more successful than himself could question his judgment and perspective, but on that stage there was no career, there wasn't even a Robert Duvall—there was only Teach, the gutter rat whose rage reached out across the footlights to grip the attention of his audience.

While he was giving his riveting performances onstage, Duvall's life offstage was not without its excitement. He was always happiest when there was one woman on whom he could concentrate his attentions, and he had found her in Lindsay Crouse. Lindsay was a gifted young woman in her late twenties who had graduated from Radcliffe with honors. She came from a prestigious New York family, all of whom were writers. Her father, Russel Crouse, was a play-wright whose collaboration with Howard Lindsay had produced the famous play *Life with Father*. Her mother, Anna Crouse, was the successful author of a series of children's books and her brother Timothy was a political writer. Lindsay, named after her father's collaborator, had grown up in a casually luxurious environment. Her parents' spacious apartment on Manhattan's Upper East Side was an informal salon for glittering talents from New York's literary and theatrical worlds. When she met Duvall, Lindsay had a budding acting career. She had gotten good reviews in the play *Between the Lines* and in *Slap Shot,* a movie about hockey life.

The attraction between Lindsay and Duvall was electric. He was intrigued with this intellectual young woman with her classical education, impressive background, and vibrant ambition, and she was delighted with his earthy directness and offhand charm. They were an attractive pair, the balding actor in such excellent physical shape who had the lead in a Broadway play and a substantial movie career, and the brainy young woman, her strong features framed by close-cropped hair. They didn't go in for a glamorous social life, though. Duvall spent scarcely any time in his cluttered pad. He took his naps and got his mail in his dressing room at the theater and visited Lindsay in her cozy apartment, a few blocks from his on the Upper West Side. They listened to country and western records, dined on prime steak, and enjoyed country weekends of jogging and playing tennis. Bobby was teaching Lindsay the game and she was doing quite well at it because her earlier training as a dancer had given her excellent footwork.

Despite their preference for privacy, they were attracting enough attention to be asked questions about their relationship. Their public statements reflect his reserve about commitment and her gushing passion for him:

> He: *I like to pal around with one woman, not a bunch. She's a good friend—and good in the other department.*
> She: *It's the best thing that ever happened to me.*
> He: *I like having her around with the guys.*
> She: *We're madly in love.*

Lindsay was lovely, but Bobby wasn't ready to tie a permanent knot again. David Mamet, however, was. The playwright had had a crush on Lindsay since he'd seen her in *Slap Shot.* Now he got to see her around the theater where his play was being performed almost every night—waiting for Bobby Duvall.

It was a very exciting time for Mamet. His newest play, *A Life in the Theater,* was playing in Chicago, and an old play of his, *Sexual Perversity in Chicago,* was at the Cherry Lane Theater in Greenwich Village, while *American Buffalo* was on Broadway. Mamet, who the year before had won the 1976 Obie (Off-Broadway) Award as the best new American playwright of the year, was attracting all sorts of attention. Not all of it was positive, though. A lot of the critics had trouble with *American Buffalo.* They felt it didn't have enough of a plot and found the language offensive. The language *was* pretty rough, so much so that Duvall had asked his parents not to come to see it because he was certain the gutter phrases would offend them. The admiral said that having commanded a ship he'd heard everything, but Bobby was adamant and the senior Duvalls bowed to his judgment and had to forego the pleasure of seeing their son in one of his most engrossing roles.

Mamet could take heart, though, from those critics who

saw in the hoodlums' colorful language a new kind of poetry, expressive of deeply felt emotion in people who, although uneducated, possess a vivid verbal repertoire. His confidence about his work may have inspired Mamet to confidence in more personal areas. Exactly what happened is something that only the three of them know. While speculation is infinite, the facts are simple. In June 1977, Duvall's run in *American Buffalo* ended. In October of that year Lindsay Crouse opened in New Haven in two short David Mamet plays, *Reunion* and *Dark Pony*. Two months later, David Mamet and Lindsay Crouse were married, and Lindsay Crouse Mamet had the distinction of being probably the only person in the world who carried the names of three playwrights in her own. She continued her acting career and eventually she and Mamet moved to a house in Vermont and had a baby. They are known as a very close couple who are a tremendous help to each other in their work.

Duvall was back on his own again, with that nervous sense of being on the prowl that he had never liked. *American Buffalo* had brought a mixed return for his investment of time and the financial sacrifice it entailed. The play was neither a commercial nor a total critical success. But Duvall's performance had received significant praise, and the project had been an immensely artistically rewarding one for him. Now he needed money again because his impending divorce was bound to be a costly experience. He had signed to play a part in the upcoming film *The Betsy*. The script was weak, but the price was attractive, as was the fact that Laurence Olivier would be in the picture, too.

Just as his run in *American Buffalo* was coming to a close, Duvall had the enormously gratifying experience of seeing one of his most cherished projects come to fruition when *We're Not the Jet Set* opened in New York. Duvall had finished the film back in 1974, but it had taken three more years to get together enough money to finance an opening at a commercial theater. The year it was finished he had shown it at a two-day film festival in December 1974 at the Fifth Avenue Cinema under the auspices of the Association of Independent Video and Film Makers, and in England, where it won the London Film Festival Award.

The unpretentious documentary opened at New York's Film Forum in June for a two-weekend run, and at the New Yorker Theater in July for a regular engagement. While it evoked some critical interest, this minimal exposure did nothing to recoup the hundreds of thousands of dollars the film had cost Duvall. But it was fascinating to see the effect this film, which pulled no punches about rodeo life, had on the New York critics.

It had long been Duvall's contention that the Westerns ground out by Hollywood in no way resembled life as it was really lived in cattle country. With his own film, he wanted to show how it truly is, stripped of all the frills and contrived glamour. And that's what he accomplished, taking the urban audiences aback by the harsh reality of what they saw on the screen.

"Unveils a cruel but authentic life-style," said Tom Allen in *The Soho Weekly News*. "Not a pretty picture, but definitely worth a visit," wrote David Sterritt in *The Christian Science Monitor*. "What really distinguishes the picture is Duvall's affinity and concern," noted Stanley Kauffmann in *The New Republic*.

The roughneck Petersons with their brawling, their drinking, their cattle branding and gelding, and their virulent male chauvinism came as something of a shock to people raised on more traditional cowboy fare, but they had to admit that the picture was relentlessly realistic and full of a colorful, if not always comfortable, energy.

After the opening at the New Yorker, Duvall invited family, friends, and press to a party at the cameraman's home. It was like a reunion: his parents were there; his brothers; Barbara, who was listed on the credits as the producer; and her girls, who had worked hard on the film during those weekends of shooting in Nebraska.

The late Arthur Bell, the witty columnist from *The Village Voice,* was there: he had liked the film, although he said that he would prefer the jet set. "If Sam Peckinpah were to go for cinema verité, this is the movie he'd make" was the way Bell put it. The chatty columnist interviewed Rear Admiral Duvall and asked him if those macho scenes were anything like his famous son's childhood. The senior Duvall didn't think they were, but did say that Bobby had been "very competitive from the time he was a little tot, particularly in sports. His efforts to excel have made him the best tennis player in Hollywood, as well as an excellent character actor," said the proud father.

It was an evening rich with the pride of accomplishment. Duvall was gratified that he'd been able to bring his pet project before the public, even on so limited a basis. It had been a tremendous experience, but a very costly one. His career as a producer-director had to be over. It simply wasn't practical, and at forty-six a man needs to be practical. No more making his own movies, Duvall promised himself.

8

ANGELO, THEIR LOVE

Duvall broke that promise to himself a very short time later. He turned the corner on his Upper West Side block, and there was this small, swarthy boy with beguiling dark eyes handing out leaflets for a fortune teller and quarreling with a grown-up woman.

"If you don't love me no more, Patricia, I'm gonna move to Cincinnati."

Duvall knew he would have to find out more about this urchin who could deliver so unique an ultimatum. And that's how as improbable a figure as a gypsy boy moved into Robert Duvall's life.

Angelo Evans, then seven years old, lived just a few doors down from Duvall's apartment building. Everyone on the block knew him because he was always on the street passing out those fliers for his mother, Mrs. Ruthie, the palm reader. Extraordinarily precocious, Angelo was a great favorite among the neighborhood women, with whom he would flirt with a street savvy far beyond his years.

Patricia Rebraca, owner of a local plant store, had a strangely compelling relationship with Angelo. He would sit on her lap for hours, gazing into her eyes, telling her he loved her, kissing her. Patricia saw herself in a maternal role with him, but their spats had the flavor of a lovers' quarrel, like the one that first intrigued Duvall.

Watching the doe-eyed boy hustling his way through the

city streets, Duvall knew he had a movie in the making, all
his resolves to be practical to the contrary. He looked at
Angelo and said to himself, "This kid has to be put in a film
because nothing like this has ever been on film before."

He got to know Angelo's family and friends, slowly ac-
quiring glimpses of the gypsy world few outsiders have ever
seen. Soon he was like one of the family, helping himself
from the refrigerator, eating the gypsy specialties like cod-
fish that Angelo's father would prepare for him. And all the
while the imaginary reel in his head kept turning with
scenes of Angelo on the screen.

First he tried the conventional route, commissioning a
script with Angelo as the central figure hitchhiking across
the country. But it wasn't right for telling about Angelo.
There had to be a more authentic vehicle. Duvall turned to
Horton Foote for advice, and the veteran screenwriter encouraged the actor to write his own script.

He turned for advice to another friend—Gail Mac-
Lachlan Youngs. Gail was John Savage's sister, and she met
Bobby when she stopped backstage at *American Buffalo* after
a performance to say hello to her brother. Savage introduced Gail to the play's star, and the chemistry started
working right away. Gail was a fledgling actress and a shel-
tered young woman in her mid-twenties who had grown up
in a comfortable Long Island suburb. The first night she
and Duvall spent together, she was too embarrassed to face
him in the morning, so she slipped out while he was in the
shower. "I'd never done anything like that before," she explained later with a blush.

Gail was wildly in love, but Bobby was cautious. He was
going through the trauma of seeing a marital separation
turn into a divorce proceeding; only a short time before
he'd broken off a live-in relationship with another ardent
young woman; and then there was his waning affair with

Lindsay Crouse. Cherishing his independence, Bobby Duvall wasn't rushing into anything.

But he kept seeing Gail and he kept sharing his *Angelo* ideas with her. It was Gail who pointed out that the anecdotes Bobby was picking up from hanging out with the gypsies were more interesting than any script could be. Why didn't he forget about a formal script and just write a skeletal story, trusting the gypsies to improvise most of the words and the action?

It was a brilliant idea because improvising comes so naturally to gypsies, whose whole history has been an improvisation. Like the rodeo circuit riders on their Nebraska ranch, the gypsies lived on the edge of excitement and danger, their styles and values rooted in another time and culture from contemporary America. Their story could best be told in their own words. Impressed with Gail's grasp of the situation, Duvall persuaded her to coproduce the picture with him.

Duvall wrote the skeletal script himself, developing the basic story line from his now intimate knowledge of gypsy mores. He'd been accepted by that clannish society to the point where he was receiving invitations to parties, weddings, and even to such secretive rites as the *kris,* a ritualized gypsy community trial, and a bride sale in which the groom's family paid $8,500 for his wife.

Duvall worked with a simple story line revolving around a ring stolen from Angelo's family and the boy's adventures in retrieving the gem. Weaving in fact and fiction, Duvall kept the basic plot flexible, subject to the same improvisation he was expecting to get in the dialogue. When he was stumped, he'd call up a gypsy friend and ask, "Now what would happen here?"

Writing days and typing nights, Duvall got the script into shape quickly. The next step was to make a sample reel to accompany the script when he made the rounds of potential investors. Working with Joseph Friedman, his cameraman on *We're Not the Jet Set,* Duvall filmed Angelo's eighth birthday party. Then he took script and reel in hand and approached the money men.

They all turned him down. He thought he was getting somewhere with a bunch of Texas tycoons, but they shook their heads over the proposed movie's lack of stars and were concerned that the gypsies, with their notorious reputation for thievery and conniving, were a poor risk and unlikely to have a commercial appeal. An Israeli businessman was willing to put up the capital, but wanted too much control over the picture in exchange for his investment. Duvall noted wryly that it was the only offer he received, and the only time he took Angelo with him when he made his pitch.

Despite his increasing preoccupation with the *Angelo* project, Duvall still had his own acting career to maintain. He made the "Ike" miniseries in the spring of 1978, and *The Great Santini* the following autumn, all the time trying to raise the money for his own picture. In the winter of 1979 he rented the house near his parents in Alexandria and spent the next several months trying to find a backer. But none was forthcoming for so risky a venture. Meanwhile, Angelo was getting bigger all the time, and his mystique was dependent on the contrast between his pint-sized body and his worldly head.

It boiled down to a simple choice: either chuck the project or finance it himself. The latter course of action was fraught with financial danger because the chance of making his money back wasn't good. But Duvall was too engrossed with his gypsies and his script to let it go. He decided to go ahead and put his checkbook on the line with his dreams. He hoped he could get by with spending $500,000 to $750,000, but these figures proved to be unrealistically low.

Back in New York, Duvall continued his investigation of gypsy customs and intrigues. His friendship with the captivating Angelo was as strong as ever. The fair actor and the swarthy boy were quite a duo, dining in chic restaurants, where Angleo would send the salad back to the kitchen if it wasn't quite to his liking, and dancing at discos, both their "dates" being women in their twenties.

As he prepared to go into production, Duvall was determined that authenticity, that elusive quality he'd fought so hard for in *Tomorrow,* would not be compromised in this picture over which he had complete control. And the means he would use to maintain authenticity was improvisation. As much as possible the gypsies would play themselves: Angelo, his brother, his mother and his father, their friends and neighbors. The plot called for a Russian gypsy car thief who would steal the ring. Instead of hiring an actor for the role, Duvall found a real Russian gypsy.

He discovered Steve "Patalay" Tsigonoff in classic Hollywood fashion, polishing his car in front of Schwab's drugstore. Duvall gave the gypsy an improvised scene to do, one in which he visits his mother's grave. Steve simulated pouring liquor on the grave and leaving cigarettes there, presents for his mother, and started to cry. Duvall knew he had a natural and signed up Steve and his sister Millie, who plays his wife in the film. The loutish, lovable pair practically stole the show with their hilarious antics, like stealing chickens in broad daylight. The cast was now complete, including two bit parts—opera singers in a restaurant played by none other than Jack and Bud Duvall. Shooting was ready to begin early in 1980.

It was just as well they had decided on an improvisational approach because none of the gypsies could read or write, considering formal schooling a part of the outside world they wished to shun. Before each day's shooting Duvall would explain the situation with story points and tag lines, after which the gypsies would improvise the scene and the dialogue. "Next movie I make, I'm going to *read* the script," Angelo declared after a particularly trying take.

Angelo was as infuriating as he was appealing. He would show up hours late, accustomed to sleeping until noon, and would stalk off the set when something displeased him. But he was thrilled the first time he saw himself in the rushes. "Bobby, I *love* myself!" he exclaimed with his usual lack of inhibition.

Duvall, who had so often been temperamental with directors he found intrusive, was now in the position of having to soothe ruffled feathers on both the frustrated crew and the impatient gypsies. The American technicians had a hard time getting used to this working method where no daily shot list existed, nor was there any guarantee that the disorganized cast would even show up. The gypsies, on the other hand, couldn't take too much routine or structure.

Fortunately, Duvall's cameraman, Joseph Friedman, worked very smoothly with the director and was able to tailor the working conditions to suit the gypsy temperament. Friedman refrained from using lights that were too hot because the undisciplined cast wouldn't tolerate that much discomfort. He worked quickly because they weren't able to handle long delays. In return for his accomodating flexibility, Friedman was given a wide latitude and a high degree of creative freedom. "Bobby is not specific about setting up shots," Friedman has explained. "He was trusting, leaving most of the technique to me while he worried about the performances."

Duvall agrees with this assessment. "Basically I am not very technical. . . . I wasn't interested in how the camera moved, as long as it captured the behavior and the story line—Angelo as he slips through life knowing, using, and forgetting people."

This quick characterization of his young friend shows how objective Duvall was about Angelo. He neither condemned nor condoned the gypsy way of life; he observed and recorded it. Parts of their value system he could admire: "The joy of knowing these people is feeling their sense of freedom. You take that away, and you wouldn't have the same people." But he had no illusions about them. "Gypsies like to throw curves—just for fun," he realized. Speaking of the 20,000 to 50,000 gypsies in New York, he explained: "They're cut from a different moral fabric. They pay no taxes, they record no births."

Duvall knew the gypsies well enough to know that only the improvisational techniques, the flexible mental set, would be effective in portraying their mercurial lives. He accepted the fact that the staccato rhythm of their existence would intrude on his shooting schedule—but it was just that pattern he wanted to convey. That's why he was eager to incorporate actual events in their lives into the film despite their unpredictability. During the filming Angelo's brother got married; a month later his mother decided she wasn't satisfied with the girl's palm-reading technique, so she sent her back to Detroit, disconcerting the crew, who had already shot two scenes with the defunct bride.

Patience, never a strong point with Duvall, was a trait he had to cultivate to maneuver the varied crises that erupted on the set. There was the time he was working with a group of Russian gypsies. Calling for a lunch break on a day when the crew had only half an hour to set up the next scene, Bobby and Gail logically gave the order, "Crew, eat first." The gypsies went wild, the men accusing Duvall of insulting their women, the women screaming and cursing at him.

With an unaccustomed docility, Duvall went around apologizing because completing the day's shooting was more important to him than challenging these bizarre accusations.

Gail was amazed at her coproducer's forebearance that day. Sensitive and perceptive, she had as clear an understanding of the nature of the cast as Bobby had, and she developed her own technique for dealing with them: "You just have to try to take a deep breath and not try to make them the way you want them to be. Part of what makes the gypsies so special is that they have this irreverence for *everything*. They don't care, which makes them very good actors, very natural."

Naturalness was what Duvall demanded from his unique cast. "No friggin' acting," he shouted to Tsigonoff when the gypsy put too many flourishes into his performance. In the interests of spontaneity, Duvall rarely yelled "Action" when the cameras started to roll. And with all the hassles and pressures, he was very pleased with some of the rushes he was getting from his maverick leading character: "Angelo has brilliant moments in this film, things I couldn't do and he probably couldn't do again. But that's okay because that's the thing about film. You catch things and they're frozen. You got 'em. And unless something happens to the negative, you've got 'em forever."

Yes, the film was going well, but the price was mounting. By the time they'd reached the postproduction period, Duvall had run out of money. That's why he accepted a part in the movie *The Pursuit of D. B. Cooper*, starring Treat Williams as the man who bailed out of a passenger plane with $200,000 in extorted money. Duvall plays Bill Gruen, the tough insurance investigator for the airline and former Green Beret. The movie turned out to be an expensive flop, but many who saw it enjoyed the daredevil chase scenes and colorful explosions set to country music.

Angelo was very much with Duvall on the *Pursuit* set, both the boy and the film. Bobby had the young gypsy join him on location in Jackson Hole, Wyoming. Angelo made a big production of calling his mother and wailing his heart out about how homesick he was, but it turned out he hadn't even bothered to dial the number. When the location moved to Tucson, Duvall had his editor, Stephen Mack, join him there. Like Joseph Friedman, Mack had worked with Duvall on *We're Not the Jet Set* and was familiar with the kind of work the boss wanted. When *Pursuit* was finished, Duvall and Mack moved the cutting room back to New York and continued the demanding task of condensing 160,000 feet of film into a coherent movie.

The grueling postproduction took its toll on the relationship between the two producers, and they decided to call the personal part of their association quits. During the work on *Angelo,* all other considerations were put aside. When it was over the couple had to take another look at where they were. "There was a lot of tension, because I wanted to go back to acting and he was against it. He thought a woman's place should be home," Gail explains.

"If you marry an actress under thirty, she'll cook you one meal a week; if she's over thirty, it'll be two meals a week," Duvall once said in an unguarded moment of male chauvinism. Although his ex-wife had stayed home and his marriage hadn't worked out, he still clung to the notion of the stay-at-home wife. But he also wanted the woman who had worked with him so brilliantly and so diligently to make their *Angelo* dream a reality.

Bobby and Gail were apart for fourteen painful months while he thrashed out his conflicts about the kind of wife and home life he felt he had to have. During that difficult period he realized the strength of his feeling for her. In his dogged way he solved the problem in his head and came to the conclusion that it was all right for his wife to have an acting career of her own.

The husband that friends like Jimmy Caan knew existed so strongly in Bobby Duvall rose to the surface. His days of second bachelorhood and nights on the lonely prowl were over. He was ready to marry again. Bobby Duvall and Gail Youngs had shared a creative project and had gotten to know each other thoroughly. Now both of them were ready to share their lives.

They were married in August 1982 on an island off the coast of Maine near Boothbay Harbor. Set in a rugged seascape renowed for its wild beauty, the island didn't allow any cars to mar its scenic perfection. A minister was flown in by seaplane to perform the ceremony in the modest chapel. Bud and Jack Duvall sang the old wedding standard "Golden Days." The reception that followed the touching ceremony was filled with music because not only John Savage, but also his whole family, loves to sing.

Their personal happiness complete, Bobby and Gail Duvall still had to bring their *Angelo* dream to fruition. By this time the project had cost them a million dollars. Between his divorce settlement and his gypsy venture, Bobby was broke. But he did have a movie he and his bride fiercely believed in, and now they had to make others believe in it, too, if they were to find distributors for their product.

In February 1983 they took *Angelo, My Love* to the Manila Film Festival, where it was very well received. Before returning home they made a 185-mile detour to the now peaceful sands of Baler Beach, which Duvall had stormed as Colonel Kilgore in *Apocalypse Now.* It was almost seven years since he had shot that memorable scene, and all the war-torn chaos seemed far away as Bobby and his bikini-clad wife jogged on the sun-drenched beach. Shortly after that they took their treasure to the Cannes Film Festival, where

Duvall's reputation as a recluse was destroyed by his tireless round of public appearances. "We're here to find a distributor for our movie. When you're selling something you care about as much as this, you do what you have to do" was his explanation for his uncustomary publicity seeking.

Finally, the Duvalls found a distributor in Cinecom International Films. *Angelo, My Love* got its long-awaited nationwide opening. It also received the critical acclaim Bobby and Gail hoped it would get, once given the exposure it deserved.

On April 27, 1983, the day the film opened at the glamorous Lincoln Plaza I Theater, Vincent Canby lavished his praise on Duvall's creation in *The New York Times:* "Angelo is a kind of idealized sum total of all New York street kids, no matter what their ethnic backgrounds. . . . Angelo moves from glib, smart-talking self-assurance to childhood tears and back again, all in the space of a few seconds of screen time."

"Simmers and pulsates with sheerly human energy. Scruffy, funny, charming, unnerving. Duvall's rough-hewn movie is the antithesis of Hollywood's lamentably phony *King of the Gypsies,*" said *Newsweek.*

The Duvalls were ecstatic. Now they could get out of the debt into which their *Angelo* expenditures had thrown them. But, even more important to them, their artistic judgment and creative intuition had been vindicated. Of course, no one was more pleased with *Angelo's* success than the film's star, who, now entering adolescence, had lost none of his brash charm and hustling mentality.

He had moved with his family to an apartment in the Bronx and still pursued the pleasures of life as he chose. He would make the rounds of the discos he'd once visited with Bobby and then take a taxi home, getting to sleep around 3 A.M. and waking up in time for the soaps. Duvall and Gail kept in touch with him. "I told him," Duvall says, "'Angelo, if you're going to be an actor, you have to learn to read and write.' But they're not used to any regimentation. Gypsies live the way they want to live. Angelo told me: 'Americans work Monday, Tuesday, Wednesday, Thursday, and Friday and have Saturday and Sunday off. With us, we have every day off. We're free.'"

Caught between the gypsy and American worlds, Angelo isn't quite sure which direction he'll take. He's aware of the conflict and puts it in his own inimitable way: "You drink a little Pepsi; you drink a little Coke. You get two flavors out of life. But I'll never lose touch with the gypsies. I can go to them and they'll always give me a chair to sit down on."

Angelo, My Love may turn out to have been a flash in the pan of a gypsy street hustler's life or it may have had the effect of giving Angelo Evans a direction he couldn't have otherwise found. It's too soon to tell; after all, Angelo is still in his early teens. But for Bobby and Gail Duvall, the film had an inestimable effect on their lives. For one thing, it brought them together. As attracted as he was to Gail initially, Bobby might not have overcome his fear of another commitment were it not for observing Gail's warmth, sensitivity, integrity, and loyalty as they made their movie together. For Gail, the picture was not only a chance to prove herself to the man she loved, but also a vehicle for her to enter the movie industry. It provided a rare opportunity for a novice to quickly develop a vast array of skills and talents. It increased her self-confidence immeasurably and was a catalyst to her professional ambition.

Angelo, My Love gave Bobby Duvall what amounted to a second career. He'd cut his directorial teeth on *We're Not the Jet Set,* but that documentary of Nebraskan ranchers was a far more modest production than the gypsy picture. *Angelo* got the distribution and attention unavailable to *Jet Set* and firmly established its director's reputation.

He'd seen it through from the scripting to the shooting to the editing to the search for a reliable distributor. From a street scene that struck his fancy to openings in prominent movie theaters in major American cities, Duvall had kept faith with his concept of what the movie should be. He'd proven that an improvisational scripting is feasible and that the camera can record the actions of real people without distorting or glamorizing or romanticizing them.

But he didn't want to turn his back on acting for directing. He saw the two disciplines interacting to make him better at both of them. Watching the gypsies give their uninhibited performances was a very personal kind of inspiration to him: "Seeing that kind of pure acting every day on the set reinforced my own ideas about acting. It forced me to say to myself, 'If they can do it, then I must keep doing it.' There are people who don't appreciate that or don't think that's what acting is all about, but for me that's what it's all about."

But he didn't think in terms of a conventional directing career. "I would like to direct films outside the establishment," he explained after the opening of *Angelo, My Love,* "and act within the establishment. I want my films to be under my control. I want the final say and the final cut because I want a different kind of film than Hollywood puts out, and I don't know how much control they allow you in Hollywood."

If he chooses to direct another film, Duvall will undoubtedly choose another subject from that underside of contemporary American culture that he finds so fascinating. Gypsies, like cowboys, live with a flamboyant style outside the limitations imposed on people with more conventional lives. The B. A. Peterson family intrigued Duvall because, so authentically western, they were remote from the Hollywood version of themselves. In the same way, Angelo's people captured his imagination because they were so different from anything that had ever been filmed before. They were the most authentic of street people, and that's where he filmed them—on their steets, speaking their argot, using their natural gestures, expressions, and interactions.

Angelo, My Love ends with a gypsy epitaph Duvall once saw on a tombstone: "Sometimes you get the bear; sometimes the bear gets you." He says he isn't clear as to its meaning because after five years spent with the gypsies and making a movie with them, he still doesn't really understand them.

It's that touch of mystery that gives his film its charm. It doesn't analyze or hypothesize; it just pulls a curtain aside and gives the audience a peek into another world. Maybe the bear is whatever you want it to be. Perhaps for Robert Duvall the bear was the compromises that he had to make in so many pictures—the crucial scenes cut, the bowing to commercial interests and popular tastes that gnaw away at creative integrity. With *Angelo, My Love,* Duvall got the bear. There were no compromises with his artistic standards, or with his commitment to authenticity and his use of improvisational techniques. He put his personal financial security on the line—and the gamble paid off. And that's an exhilarating feeling for anyone, be he a gypsy, an actor, or a director.

9

CONFESSIONS IN LOW KEY

Another effect his experience as a director had on Duvall the actor was the determination to make more money in the latter profession. His attitude about the business end of moviemaking had always been careless. For the most part he was content with the second lead if he found it meatier than the lead. Duvall's long-time friends were well aware of his disregard for calculated career planning. He had waved aside Dustin Hoffman's hard-nosed advice that he concentrate more on the practical aspects of an acting career. Ulu Grosbard once noted that "Bobby, in a strange way, did not devote a great deal of energy to the career aspects of his work. He would just go with whatever instinct he had at the moment. Acting wasn't a business to him. He wasn't making sure that the next step was the right step."

Still, there was an ambivalence in Robert Duvall about success. Anyone as competitive about sports as he is couldn't look at the commercial triumphs of his old friends without making some comparisons. He would grumble to Paul Gleason about why Hackman and Caan were getting so much more for their roles than he was for his. Gleason would explain that Caan had a public relations man, that he gave lots of interviews and took great care with his image. Bobby knew that wasn't for him, but still it hurt sometimes.

There were other hurts, like the fact that the villain role in the 1972 screen version of *Wait Until Dark* went to Alan

Arkin and not to him who had played it so brilliantly on Broadway. There had been the disappointment of being turned down for the part of Woody Guthrie in *Bound for Glory* because he was considered too old. Some of his career decisions didn't have too much consistency. He turned down the lead in *Jaws,* for instance, because he was after the part of the shark hunter instead; but then he turned down the country singer role in *Nashville* because he wasn't of-fered enough money.

Then came the double drain on his income, having to pay the hefty alimony Barbara was demanding and needing to finance his gypsy movie. Duvall realized that if he wanted to continue to live in the easy style to which he'd grown accus-tomed and also to be able to indulge his taste for turning quirky subjects into documentaries or feature films, he'd have to take the business aspects of his career more se-riously.

He needed a business manager he could trust. The slick Hollywood agents weren't for him; their approach to his ca-reer alienated him and elicited his stubborn streak. He needed someone who spoke his language, appreciated his expectations and reservations—someone who knew him well. Bobby found that person in his younger brother, Jack.

The three Duvall brothers had remained close, but couldn't see one another as often as they liked. Bud lived with his family in Milwaukee, where he was a professor of music at the University of Wisconsin, while Jack made his home in Alexandria and practiced law in the Washington area. When the three of them did get together, though, there was as much music and mimicry and laughter as ever. Bobby got to see a lot more of Jack than he had since their boyhood when he rented the house in Alexandria in the winter of 1979 following the shooting of *The Great Santini.*

By the fall of that year he had faced the fact that no one

but himself was going to be willing to finance the *Angelo* venture. Mulling over matters with Jack, Bobby decided to place his career, his business, and his legal affairs in his brother's highly competent hands. The choice turned out to be a very wise one. Jack took an overall view of his brother's career and saw what needed work.

For one thing, his image. Jack thought Bobby had played too many bad guys. "If that label gets attached to you," he said, "you don't have as much choice or movement in parts." He wanted to see his new client avoid bad-guy typecasting, and take more cognizance of the "commercial potential" of pictures proposed to him. Jack knew Bobby needed someone to push for lead roles for him and was aware of how important it was for his fiercely independent brother to have the right to approve the directors of his movies. Knowing Bobby's carelessness in business matters, Jack insisted on his having the right to inspect the financial accounts of films in which he had a piece of the action.

The first significant film Duvall made under this new regime of career management was *True Confessions,* which was released in 1981, *The Pursuit of D. B. Cooper,* also released that year, having been simply a means to quickly raise the cash he needed for the postproduction work on *Angelo, My Love.* When Duvall first read the script he wasn't particularly keen on taking the part of Tom Spellacy. But because Ulu Grosbard, with whom he'd so far worked only on the stage, would be directing the film, he gave it his serious consideration. Grosbard was convinced that the Spellacy role was as right for Duvall as Teach in *American Buffalo* had been. Then Jack adroitly negotiated a fee of $750,000 for his brother, the highest sum he'd ever been paid for any movie. That clinched it for Bobby. For once artistic and commercial interests seemed to be converging.

If ever a movie started out as a mutual admiration society,

it was *True Confessions.* Duvall explained that he took the part because of Grosbard. "He lets an actor alone. He can handle someone improvising. You've got to wing it in acting. Things happen that can't be preset. I'm an actor who can improvise. A director who can allow that to happen a little, that is good."

Grosbard said that one of the reasons De Niro did the film was to work with Duvall. "I know he admires his work tremendously, and they worked well together. I think that's because they're going for the same thing. They respond to the moment. They have no preconceptions that cut them off. They are both exceptionally alive and spontaneous."

De Niro and Duvall sharing top billing in an intensely introspective portrait of two brothers was enough to whet any movie buff's appetite. Although they had both been in *Godfather II,* they'd had no scenes together; now they would be sharing emotion-charged encounters. They were perceived as belonging to the same school of acting, which sharpened Hollywood's curiosity about how they would interact on the screen. While *The Great Santini,* although hardly a blockbuster, had given Duvall some needed box office appeal, De Niro was far more widely known. His portrayals of the violence-prone cabbie in *Taxi Driver,* the macho steelworker turned soldier in *The Deer Hunter,* and the notorious, frenzied middleweight boxing champion Jake La Motta in *Raging Bull* were widely acclaimed as monumental performances.

If there was one actor who was as thorough and meticulous in prepping for a role as Robert Duvall, it was Robert De Niro. In *Raging Bull* he had had none other than Jake La Motta himself as his technical assistant, putting him through the paces to prepare for the fight scenes. Now, still overweight from the seventy extra pounds he'd put on to look like the prizefighter in his later years, De Niro had the technical assistance of a priest to help him with *True Confessions*. The Reverend Henry Fehran was sufficiently impressed with the actor's zeal in learning the priestly trappings to remark, "How holy we would be if we worked as conscientiously [as De Niro did for the part] at becoming saints."

While De Niro was learning the mass in Latin and the correct way to don vestments, Duvall was visiting the city morgue with Grosbard and hanging around the Los Angeles police stations, talking to the detectives to get a better handle on Tom Spellacy, the hard-boiled, cynical cop whose investigation of a murder turns up evidence of the corruption surrounding his ambitious brother, Monsignor Des Spellacy.

Duvall's scenes in *True Confessions* had something of a reunion about them. His muted romantic interest in the film was Brenda Samuels, a weary former Hollywood madam played by Grosbard's wife, Rose Gregorio, with whom Duvall had last acted almost twenty years earlier when they had portrayed the youthful provincials in Manhattan in *The Days and Nights of Beebee Fenstermaker*.

His sturdy sidekick in the film was Kenneth McMillan, with whom he had played in *American Buffalo,* also under Grosbard's direction. And, of course, there was the actor whose performance as the young Vito Corleone Duvall had watched with such admiring interest. Duvall and De Niro—the results should have been dynamic. Some found them so; others not at all.

Few movies have ever evoked as wide a spectrum of critical evaluation as *True Confessions*. The screenplay was the work of John Gregory Dunne, author of the novel from which it was adapted, and his wife, the novelist Joan Didion. In his scathing *Time* magazine review, Richard Corliss wondered if the problems in the picture could be attributed to

Ms. Didion's participation in the project, referring to her as the "Empress of Angst." Corliss complained that "onscreen characters who should percolate with rage simply simmer . . . Duvall spends too much time pacing and waiting; De Niro's big scene has him hanging up vestments."

Many critics raised the objection that the film was too much of a tease, promising a macho detective yarn with a hard-edged-LA-in-the-late-1940s-ambience, but then failing to deliver that kind of punch. Many felt it also failed in its endeavor to be an in-depth probe into the nature of human corruption as it affects a complex relationship between two brothers.

"This is a very odd movie: it attempts to be both a *Chinatown* and an Irish *Godfather*," Pauline Kael tartly observed in *The New Yorker*. Kael also took exception to Grosbard's directing: "For actors it's probably bliss to work with Ulu Grosbard because he encourages them to take time and space . . . he appears to be a serious director who lacks a film sense. He simply has no feeling for the vital energies that propel a movie. Essentially he makes films by photographing the performances of actors whom he admires." *Variety* shared Kael's objections to Grosbard's direction, calling it a "muted, unmuscular telling of the sordid fateful events."

But others saw a discerning directorial hand in the praiseworthy performances. "Grosbard has helped Duvall build the anger from a buried agony," Stanley Kauffmann observed in *The New Republic*, writing a thoughtful article entitled "Waiting for Grosbard" in which he speculated that the director's full ability had not yet been utilized in the cinema medium. Kauffmann noted that "Duvall is again slow-fused dynamite, with his little smiles of anger or disgust, his hesitations, his half-glances away."

Another critic impressed with Duvall's performance was

The Village Voice's iconoclastic Andrew Sarris, who speculated that "it is possible to and pleasant to anticipate that *True Confessions* might do for Duvall's career what *Midnight Cowboy* did for Jon Voight's—move him into the league of powerhouse leads. Duvall's scenes with Rose Gregorio generate a tenderness and a pathos I have never associated with this non-woman-oriented actor." Sarris sums up the film as being "all in all a dazzling display from Duvall, a solid and subtle contribution from De Niro, and an honorable and adult piece of filmmaking from Grosbard, Dunne, and Didion."

Rex Reed couldn't have agreed less with Sarris, stating in his *Daily News* review: "Good as both actors are, I felt while watching their mush-mouthed histrionics that I was listening to a short-wave radio underwater. . . . This movie is so unnecessarily confusing, so overbearingly hysterical, and so disturbingly incoherent that it took me nearly an hour to figure out what was going on. . . . The actors are even less coherent than the plot. There's De Niro whispering piously through his stoic double chins, with Duvall on the other side of the screen, swallowing his tongue and mumbling inaudibly, both of them overacting like crazy. The poor audience, fearing communal hearing disorders, ends up the victim."

And then for the other side of the critical debate is Archer Winsten in the *New York Post*, saying, "The performances of Robert De Niro and Robert Duvall are so intense and fascinating that they would overshadow the movie itself if the actors weren't so deeply immersed in their roles."

The De Niro and Duvall performances exerted a fascination for the critics, who, whether they admired their skill or questioned their effectiveness, had strong opinions on them. Writing in *The San Francisco Chronicle*, Peter Stack found De Niro "unusually devoid of flamboyance and machismo," and saw Duvall as "the Monsignor's crude and alienated brother, the contemptible Irishman who, with smirk and jaded eyes, has visited all of life's dirty streets and whose volatile nature has deprived him of social standing and a family."

Perhaps it was because the critics and public were used to seeing De Niro in much more flamboyant roles that they tended to dismiss his performance as too low-key, while they were more intrigued by Duvall's, whose talents they were really just beginning to recognize.

In an article in *New York* magazine, "The Secret Stardom of Robert Duvall," film critic William Wolf gave an insightful evaluation of Duvall's career as it stood in 1981 when *True Confessions* was released: "Duvall has been called 'America's premier actor' and 'America's Olivier,' but so far he has still not become a bankable superstar. He has been dogged by the perception that he is a character actor instead of a leading man. But by strictly artistic standards, Duvall already *is* a superstar and has been one for years."

Wolf defined Duvall's artistry as "the authenticity he manages to bring to his roles. He has an uncanny ability to make his characters utterly convincing. They don't just appear— they come from somewhere, they have pasts. In *True Confessions,* Duvall makes you feel as if there is nothing his cop has not seen and heard during his years on the force. It is not easy to upstage Robert De Niro, who plays Spellacy's brother, a monsignor whose wheeling and dealing for the church criss-crosses with Spellacy's relentless investigation of a murder. But at times in this film, Duvall does it."

But according to Vincent Canby, who had bestowed that "America's Olivier" accolade on Duvall, it was not a question of upstaging but of creative cooperation: *"True Confessions,"* Canby wrote in an article in *The New York Times* that was a follow-up to his original review of the film, "is, further, a celebration of the entire American acting profession. To watch Mr. Duvall and Mr. De Niro together is to be treated to the kind of spectacle that is rare in movies. We respond simultaneously to what each actor is doing in his role within the movie as well as to the exalting surprises that come when we recognize an actor hitting a nuance, or a level of performing, never before revealed in his other films. . . . I'm not talking about the bravura performing of the sort that distinguished Mr. De Niro's work in *Raging Bull* or Mr. Duvall's in *The Great Santini*, but of ensemble acting. Neither actor has ever been better, though each has been far more flamboyant. They play together with an intensity and intelligence that illuminate the film as well as the performances of the hugely gifted cast of supporting actors."

So the critical debate raged on, with the pros talking about the exalted performances and the cons complaining about how tedious the performances were and how the picture didn't come off as either detective genre or psychological drama.

One of the most thoughtful and most negative reviews came from Pauline Kael, who, after her initial designation of the film as "very odd" and her critique of the directing, went on to the characterizations: "A scene in which the two brothers go to visit their senile, childish mother, who's still playing little catechism games, suggests the background of their rivalry. But when they're together everything is internalized. Tom is so locked in that we never get to see how he feels about Des, and De Niro's role is so underwritten that Des doesn't particularly react to Tom, or to anything else."

Kael was astute enough to see that if there were a flaw in the performances, it might well stem from the script. The problem could be that the motivations are somewhat shrouded and that both of the actors used a similar understated style so that the combined effect was too stultifying.

Neither part is sufficiently fleshed out in the screenplay, and neither actor embellishes what is there because each is playing in a low-key mode. Kael credits Duvall with being "a formidable technician, and as Tom he's up there on the screen tense and glaring—a pair of sunken eyes in a death's head. But Duvall is working under a considerable handicap: if an actor isn't given the center of his character—if he isn't given any human motivation—what can he build the character on?"

If she had just stopped there, Kael would have been giving Duvall a positive review, crediting him with doing the best he could with a script that didn't supply him with sufficient motivation to go on. But she didn't stop there. That spirited and influential critic took her review of *True Confessions* as an opportunity to offer some comments about the general quality of Duvall's acting, pursuing the same line of thought she had started in her review of *The Great Santini* the year before. In the earlier review she had speculated that Duvall could be "one of those actors who are stars when they play character parts (as in *Apocalypse Now*) but character actors when they play star parts; some element of excitement seems to be missing—we don't have star empathy with him."

"Duvall has a deficiency as a star," Kael maintained in her *True Confessions* review. "We watch the performance objectively, *as* a performance—we don't have any special empathy with him. . . . Duvall is in some special sense an anonymous, selfless actor. We perceive a 'self' in most stars; we don't in Duvall, nor do we want to. There are roles he can do perhaps better than anyone else and without strain—in 'Ike' on television, for example. But you can see the confines of each role he plays; he's not an actor who fills out a part and spills over the edges. Nothing flows out of him. When he plays a short-tempered Irishman like Tom

Spellacy, there's nothing in his face *but* anger and tension. Aridity in an American actor is so rare that people may mistake Duvall's control for greatness, but he never gets to the point where technique is subsumed and instinct takes over."

Of course this assessment enraged Duvall. When asked about Kael's comments in a *Rolling Stone* interview, he reacted with "cold fury" to her suggestion that in *True Confessions* he had been poorly directed by Ulu Grosbard. Emphatically, Duvall stated that Grosbard is "one of the best damned directors around today. I mean, he's going to be known as much as Coppola or any of the rest of them. He understands that things have to be lifelike. Like pauses. There are pauses in life, you see, when you and I are talking, and there are beats in scenes that really make them work. He gives his actors freedom to do things. You have to have that. I can't work with any director who doesn't let me have some say about the lines, about the shaping of the scenes, who won't let me talk to the other actors, you see? That's very important. And he's good on all these counts, and for her to say what she said about the acting in *True Confessions* is ridiculous."

Duvall went on to question how critics have the audacity to tell actors how to perform. "Each critic ought to be made to make a half-hour film that would have to be shown in public. Kael. Rex Reed. There was this writer, Susan Sontag . . . she made some films, and afterward, she wrote that she wasn't going to criticize films anymore because she finally realized the tremendous difficulties the people on the periphery can't even know."

"Are you saying that Kael doesn't have the right to comment on your performance?" asked his interviewer.

"No, of course she has the right. But she really knows so little about it. Films or acting. She has one thing really—a good writing style. The truth is, I'm too good for her. She doesn't have the intelligence or ability to ruin me. I know what I'm doing; she does not know what I do. She just has an opinion. It's very subjective. I mean, if a guy runs the hundred in 9.1, how can you say he's not fast? Well, I've run some 9.1 hundreds in my time."

With his feisty nature and the firmness of his belief in his own talent, Duvall could take Kael's criticisms in stride. He responded with a natural enough anger but without self-doubt, and his innate confidence and optimism protected him from negative feelings about his work. The question of the validity of Kael's remarks remains of interest to anyone who has seriously followed Duvall's unique career. As he wisely pointed out, "It's very subjective."

Kael's reviews make fascinating reading and she is always thought-provoking and original in her responses to the films she sees. But ultimately moviegoers will make their own evaluation of an actor's abilities, and the great majority of reputable film critics would disagree with Kael's viewpoint.

One of these is, of course, Vincent Canby. In that same review in which he called Duvall "America's Olivier" after seeing *The Great Santini,* Canby made the following astute observation: "Though there are obvious, clearly defined contrasts between the Duvall performances in *The Seven-Per-Cent Solution* and *The Great Santini,* there is also a continuity that has to do with more than a recognizable physical presence. It has to do, I think, with our awareness of the power within the actor, which one comes to know only over a period of time, so that we finally understand how the actor is using that power in any given role, whether he's playing the one outsider inside the Mafia, in the *Godfather* movies, or a Detroit automotive tycoon in *The Betsy.*"

Where Kael sees Duvall lacking in the star quality that spills over from one role into another, Canby sees the sheer force of his talent as a continuity from one role to another. It is, indeed, very subjective. Canby's evaluation of Duvall is similar to the one Herbert Ross, who directed *The Seven-Per-Cent Solution,* has given: "Robert Duvall is the premier American actor. He has the power to alter himself in order to become the character he is playing. The only challenger for this nomination is George C. Scott. Only Duvall and Scott have the range and variety of Laurence Olivier."

The comparison with Scott was also made by Stanley Kauffmann, Duvall's admiring critic in *The New Republic.* In his 1977 review of *The Eagle Has Landed,* Kauffmann praised Duvall in terms few were using back then: "There's no point in listing all the other kinds of roles that Duvall has played—well. He now stands just below George C. Scott in the roster of present-day American actors: below Scott, I would say, because though he has a wider mimetic range than Scott has yet shown, he lacks Scott's force and forceful personality. Everything that Scott does is colored by Scott himself even while he authenticates his characters. Everything that Duvall does is the character only. (Yes, *only*—marvelously though he does it.) It's the difference between Gielgud and Guinness."

Through his praise Kauffmann is expressing Kael's question about Duvall's star potential. "Star" has many connotations. These critics are not talking about Hollywood hype images ground out by public relations agencies, nor even about a personality around which movie roles are tailored. What they're talking about is a quality that a few performers exude in front of the camera, an aura unique to that person that permeates the atmosphere surrounding each part they play.

Duvall does seem to lack that quality. He's the craftsman par excellence, the continuity of his identity from picture to picture deriving, as Canby says, from the public's awareness of his inner power. But he doesn't have that spillover Kael requires, that forceful personality Kauffmann sees Scott project regardless of the role he's playing. Nor would he want it. Duvall's artistic trademark has been his rare gift for getting inside the character he's playing to the point where Duvall the actor has no identity of his own on the stage or screen. For him, part of being an actor is the obliteration of his own personality in favor of the one he's portraying.

While the critics could go on debating the relative merits of Duvall's greatness, he wanted to go on making movies, always searching for the complex roles, the ones with those juicy but subtle contradictions of personality and motivation. *True Confessions* didn't do for his career what admirers like Andrew Sarris had hoped it would. He played Tom Spellacy tough and embittered, jittery with fermenting anger and unresolved animosities. Some critics were awed by his performance, while others felt it was too muted or mannered—or that the writing and direction didn't supply him with enough motivation to make a riveting character. So instead of being Duvall's vehicle for the final push to enormous success and widespread recognition, the Tom Spellacy role became one more in a stream of tough guys wearing their rage on their frayed sleeves whom Duvall has played so masterfully.

Where should he go from here? With *True Confessions* behind him, did he want another tough guy? Maybe it was time for a tender guy, of which he'd played all too few. If he could find the right tender guy in a movie of considerable merit, now that might really have possibilities. But who was the guy, and where was his movie?

10

TENDER MERCIES ARE HARD WON

The guy was Mac Sledge, and the movie was an original Horton Foote screenplay—a big inducement to Duvall, who had done what he considered his best work in the Foote adaptations of *To Kill a Mockingbird* and *Tomorrow*. Now here was a part Foote had written with his favorite actor and old friend in mind. The playwright took his script to Philip and Mary Ann Hobel, a couple who had produced over 200 documentaries between them, sensing that their touch would fit the standards of authenticity he and Duvall insisted on.

The Hobels took one look at the script and knew this was the one they wanted for their debut as theatrical film producers. They then went to EMI films, a British production company that agreed to provide financing for the film based on the script and Robert Duvall's participation, providing the Hobels could find the right director.

Duvall's days of working with directors he found unsympathetic to his flexible approach and improvisational style were over. When Jack Duvall took over the management of his brother's career, the right to have a say in the choice of director was one of the terms they agreed to hold out for. Since then, Duvall had made only one picture, *True Confessions*, and the director was the one he admired the most, Ulu Grosbard. Now he had a contractual right to okay the director of the Hobels' choice.

That choice fell on Bruce Beresford, the exciting young Australian director of the dramatic Boer War picture *Breaker Morant*. They felt that his Australian background would give him a sensitivity to the rural lives in Foote's script and an appreciation of the artistic imperative to be authentic in handling the script.

Beresford was at home in Sydney with his family when he received the script, one of hundreds pouring in since the huge success of *Breaker Morant*. When he read it he knew with that same certainty the Hobels had felt that it was for him. Decisively, Beresford picked up the phone and called Barry Spikings, who runs EMI films in London, and offered to come to the United States and take a month to drive around Texas to get the feel of the land and have an opportunity to become acquainted with Horton Foote. Then, if his initial instinct proved sound—and he was convinced it would—he'd be ready to direct the picture.

Driving around the Lone Star state, the Australian was struck by how much the people living in its isolated areas resembled those in the Australian outback, just as the Texas terrain was so reminiscent of that wild continent's bush country. Beresford's sympathies were as quickened by his talks with Foote as by his views of the Texas landscape and its people; he eagerly agreed to direct *Tender Mercies*.

This time there would be no struggle with the producers and the director over such crucial matters as the shooting location. All were agreed to aim for the highest in an authentic production. With this hand-picked ensemble, the commitment to the kind of picture Duvall and Foote had always longed to make was complete. Beresford was given a free hand in the choice of cinematographer and editor, and he chose fellow Australians. The cameraman was Russel Boyd, whose credits included *Gallipoli* and two Peter Weir pictures, *Picnic at Hanging Rock* and *The Last Wave*, which had put Australia on the movie-world map: the film editor was William Anderson, who had worked with Beresford on all his feature films.

When it came to casting, it was crucial to find the right actress to play Rosa Lee, the solid young widow whose love for him, and his for her, brings about the emotional and spiritual rehabilitation of Mac Sledge, the washed-up alcoholic country and western singer. Instead of an established star, they went for an unknown. Tess Harper was a thirty-one-year-old Dallas resident for whom *Tender Mercies* was her film debut, and her first chance to support herself from acting alone, instead of having to work at a variety of tedious jobs. To play Rosa Lee's son, they selected Allan Hubbard, a sturdy blond youngster from the neighboring town of Paris, Texas. Only when they had started shooting did the adults find out that like Sonny's father in the film, Allan Hubbard's father had been killed in Vietnam.

The location had to be as authentic as the lead actress and her child. The Hobels, Beresford, Duvall, and Foote decided on Waxahachie, a small town with a typical rural Texas look to it and the logistical advantage of being only thirty miles from Dallas. *Tender Mercies* was not the only production to have seen the advantages of Waxahachie, because it turned out that Arthur Penn had filmed *Bonnie and Clyde* there. For Rosa Lee's desolate motel they found a deserted farmhouse in the middle of a prairie and constructed a few woebegone tourist cabins, a neon sign, a Coke machine, and a pair of battered gas pumps.

In the weeks before the shooting began, Duvall roamed the Texas countryside, much as he had the Mississippi counties around which *Tomorrow* was being shot a decade earlier. Soaking up the local color, he even got a job as a singer in a country pub. By the time shooting started, Duvall was totally immersed in his Texas persona.

Shooting took place in something like record time, from November 2 to December 23, 1981, with cast and crew putting in long hours seven days a week. The Australian filmmakers and the largely Dallas-based crew quickly hit it off, the good ol' boys recognizing in the Aussies kindred frontier-style spirits. They would cement their good feeling after the exhausting work hours by hanging out together and drinking lots of long necks (Texas beer).

Things weren't going as smoothly between the director and his male lead as they were with the Australians and the Texans. Beresford, although picked by Duvall's associates with his approval, was not an Ulu Grosbard or a Francis Coppola, directors who had won the freewheeling actor's intense professional admiration over years of working well together. It was inevitable that there would be initial clashes between the foreign director and the actor who'd bristled at what he considered heavy-handed direction back when he was first starting out, and who certainly was not going to bend to another's will in a picture this close to his heart. Duvall and Foote had had their troubles with independent producers and a talented director during the filming of *Tomorrow,* and Duvall was determined not to put up with anything similar at this point in his career.

The trouble started the first day of shooting when Beresford was talking to Wilford Brimley, the hefty character actor who plays Mac's former manager. The director told the outspoken actor to pick up the pace, to which Wilford retorted, "Hey, I didn't know anybody dropped it." Duvall, of course, loved that one and didn't bother to conceal his relish at the remark.

Duvall readily admits how talented Beresford is, but insists: "He has this dictatorial way of doing things with me that just doesn't cut it. Man, I have to have my freedom. Make things happen with a line change or two there." Beresford flew back to New York after a tiff with Duvall about technical delays and was ready to quit the picture. Duvall then flew to join him and they had it out, finally resolving to mend their fences and work together.

Duvall thrives on controversy. "Bruce was trying to defend his vision of the picture and I was trying to defend mine. That's good for the whole picture. You ever been on a happy set? Everybody loves one another? Then you see the final product, and whoa . . . it's a mess."

There's no question that Bobby Duvall can be infuriating for a director to work with unless it's someone who's won his confidence over a long period of time. He has a way of talking directly to the other actors, of helping them with their interpretations and deliveries, that can upset a director who is unfamiliar with Duvall's style—both so casual and so intense. Directors almost by definition see themselves as authority figures, and Duvall has too independent a spirit to allow anyone to dominate him. He insisted on that free-form give-and-take among the cast on the *Tender Mercies* set.

Besides granting Beresford his talent, Duvall has also said of the Australian: "The actors helped him tremendously. With different people, he'd have been in trouble." This is hardly an attitude to endear an actor to a director.

But Beresford had to admire the awesome strength of Duvall's acting ability: "You could ask him to do a scene five, six times, and he'd do it exactly the same way. . . . A complete professional when it came to his lines, hitting his marks."

It wasn't Duvall's technique with which Beresford had difficulty—it was the temperament, the restlessness, the resistance to what Duvall perceived was interference and to what Beresford knew was competent direction. But in the end Beresford was left with the glowing impression of Duvall's cinematic genius. "Things did get better as we went along. I have great admiration for him as an actor. He had Mac Sledge down perfectly."

He had the part down perfectly because it had been in his head for two decades, since he started making movies. He had a mission to keep the faith with the kind of people portrayed in the picture. "It's got to be real," he explained in a *Rolling Stone* interview. "That's what I'm trying to do. And that's hard. I drove over 600 miles of road in Texas listening to accents, watching how people held their bodies, talking to farmers. Man, I wanted my character to be real. But I loved it, too. I love talking to those people. You know, that's what all my acting is really about. Dignity. Trying to find the dignity in the man. Because the avarage workingman has dignity that the Hollywood establishment has overlooked. The center and especially the South of this country have been patronized and made fun of. Things like 'The Dukes of Hazzard'—man, they're the worst. If I can do anything at all in my work to show what dignity is in the comman man, then that's what my life is really about."

It's that quality of dignity that's so moving in Mac Sledge as he holds onto it and is sustained by it through the tough times when he gives up drinking and gathers the guts to make a fresh start in life. And what comes across in Duvall's performance is his robust conviction that there is something special here to convey and that he has a solemn duty to portray it with a flawless accuracy and an uncompromising authenticity. He was in his element on the Texas location because the whole experience of shooting a movie in the southwestern heartland tugged at so many of his personal roots.

First, there were the people of Texas themselves. "Maybe I'm more of a woodsman than a redneck, but I don't hate rednecks," he says. "I love certain Southerners and Texas people. On Thanksgiving Day, we all joined this family in

east Texas. They had turkey and so much Southern cooking, it was terrific. They brought out the fiddles and guitars.
They played 'Faded Love' and the kids sang, the family
sang, we all sang. You should have heard this one guy sing
to his wife. It was wonderful."

Duvall reveled in the contact with the local people on the
set of this thoroughly down-home production. Betty Buckley, who played Dixie Scott, was from Fort Worth, just thirty
miles from the Grapevine Opry, the scene of Dixie's con-
certs in the movie. On the day they shot there, her whole
family turned out and filled in as extras.

Betty Buckley turned out to have been a very clever piece
of casting. TV viewers who had seen her on the popular
series "Eight Is Enough" were in for quite a surprise at her
vivid portrayal of the flamboyant and venomous Dixie. In
the movie, Mac Sledge was married to Dixie when they were
both successful country singers and he was drinking way too
much. When he starts over again, working at Rosa Lee's
obscure motel and falling in love with her, he tells his new
love that Dixie was poison to him. Buckley's Dixie, with her
ferocity unable to conceal her pain, is an effective counter-
part to the gentle strength of Rosa Lee.

The scenes between Mac Sledge and Rosa Lee show a new
side to Duvall's acting talent—the tender lover. The second
lead never gets the girl, and Duvall had played astonishingly
few love scenes in his lengthy movie career. Of course,
Tomorrow contained some extraordinary love scenes between
Duvall and Olga Bellin, reminiscent of the silent screen because of the expressiveness in their features, the glow in
their eyes, and their wordless exchanges. But so few people
saw that picture that it didn't do anything for Duvall's image
as a man who could be romantic on the screen. In "Ike,"
Duvall and Lee Remick gave accomplished performances
depicting a powerful mutual attraction held in check be-

cause the script stayed on the tactful side of the touchy subject of wartime romance. In *True Confessions,* only as astute a critic as Andrew Sarris had noticed the new dimension his rueful scenes with Rose Gregorio elicited in Duvall, but those were so subtle, the potential for tenderness so obscured, that they could only be considered the shadow of love scenes.

Now here he was, a lover at last, an older man wooing an enchanting young widow and winning her with his quiet integrity and rough-hewn charm. Those scenes with Tess Harper must have struck somewhere at Duvall's core, this man whose own anguished loneliness was being healed by his deepening relationship with a sensitive young woman. And the scenes with Allan Hubbard in which Mac, who's lost the right to see his daughter, forms a relationship with the fatherless boy had to have hit home to a man who raised two stepdaughters.

Those tender scenes with the widow and the boy had to be intensely moving while avoiding the pitfall of sentimentality. Here Duvall's famous restraint accomplished the feat. Mac Sledge is a taciturn man, slow to express his feelings. And this nonverbal man grows in the course of the film from someone in the depths of despair to a human being redeemed through love. Duvall creates magic with his facial expressions. Mac's features soften, and an inner glow shines through them. Duvall is thoroughly believable in all the phases of Mac's character, from desperation to salvation. Scenes like these have to be underplayed or they quickly turn maudlin. Duvall does underplay them, yet there is nothing subdued about his performance because Mac's depth of feeling and complexity of emotion are conveyed to the audience with the actor's customary subtlety and insight.

The chemistry between Duvall and Tess Harper illuminated their scenes together with the glow of burgeoning love. The inexperienced young actress was in awe of the veteran actor, and he was impressed with her talent and sincerity. Like Mac Sledge, Rosa Lee is not a talkative person; her feelings must be conveyed through subtle nuances of voice and facial expression. Duvall's help to Tess in her characterization of Rosa Lee was enormous. When the picture was finished, she said that no matter what the critics wrote, she knew she was good because Duvall had given her a parting gift, a blue cowgirl shirt with a card saying, "You really *were* Rosa Lee."

And Duvall really was Mac Sledge, the musician as much as the man. *Tender Mercies* is filled with the sounds of country music, and the picture gave the actor a chance to express a side of himself he'd never fully developed. Before he started his acting career, Bodge Duvall had been known to family and friends as an extraordinary mimic and as a talented guitar player and singer of country tunes. Music was also the thread that had tied the three Duvall brothers together from earliest childhood on.

As Mac Sledge, Duvall got to play a person he might have been had he concentrated on his musical rather than his acting gifts, had he turned his sights toward the American heartland instead of to its acting centers on the two coasts. He wrote eight of the songs he sang as Mac, and his voice had an authentic country sound.

So many aspects of Robert Duvall's life were reflected in *Tender Mercies* that it's easy to see why he is so strongly identified with Mac Sledge. The picture is the story of country people and their customs, of a lonely man's discovery of love with a serene woman, of step-parenthood, and of the joys of writing and singing heartfelt country music. It is also about religious faith, something that has always remained the bedrock of the personality of a man brought up in a devout Christian household.

Tender Mercies is, in its own quietly understated manner, a film permeated with religious feeling. Rosa Lee sings in the choir of the local Baptist church and she takes Mac there, where he is able to belt out hymns with powerful feeling. When he is ready, Mac is baptized along with Sonny, and Rosa Lee is wrapped in the tender mercy of seeing both her husband and her son embrace the faith that sustained her through long widowhood.

One of the most moving scenes in the picture is when Mac's daughter, Sue Ann, played with a touching vulnerability by Ellen Barkin, comes to see him. She asks him the words to the song about the dove she vaguely remembers him singing to her when she was a child. But Mac's too choked up to say much more than that he doesn't remember any song about a dove. Then, after she leaves, the two of them having finally made emotional contact, he stands by the window and sings "On the Wings of a Dove," his voice quivering with emotion. It's a moment of almost unbearable poignancy, the love and anguish expressed in the music suffused with a religious fervor.

Tender Mercies also represented a professional landmark. Mac Sledge was the spiritual heir to Boo Radley and Jackson Fentry, Southern men, and despised outcasts who have within them wellsprings of love and devotion. Mac Sledge was a continuation of that role Duvall and Horton Foote seemed to work on once every ten years, and he is the most fully realized of the three. Because so many of Duvall's personal experiences and lifelong concerns were in Mac Sledge, it's no wonder that his performance dazzled nearly everyone who saw it. The shooting was completed just two days before Christmas 1981, and Duvall was able to return to his problem of finding a distributor for *Angelo, My Love* with a renewed sense of purpose—and to Gail Youngs, his Rosa Lee, whom he now knew he would marry. A month after their Maine island wedding, Duvall took off for Toronto in September 1982 to film *The Terry Fox Story*.

Terry Fox was a young Canadian who had lost a leg to cancer. He had died over a year earlier, midway through his attempt to run the breadth of Canada in order to stimulate contributions for cancer research. This movie about his life was the first feature-length film produced in Canada for pay-TV (HBO) in the United States. The part of Terry was played by Eric Fryer, a twenty-one-year-old Canadian who had also lost his right leg to cancer. Duvall played Bill Vigors, the public relations expert from the Canadian Cancer Society who accompanied Fox on most of his 3,339-mile run.

During the four weeks he spent in Toronto, there wasn't one flare-up of the Duvall temper on the set. In fact, the film's director, Ralph Thomas, said, "He's one of the easiest people I ever worked with," and praised the actor's enormous generosity in going out of his way "to make the kid look good."

"The kid" was Eric Fryer, who was at first shy with the famous movie actor. But Duvall quickly put him at his ease. They ran together on September 19 in the Cancer Society's fund-raising trek through Toronto, which also served as a backdrop for the picture. Duvall worked hard with Fryer on his delivery, aware of the necessity for avoiding sentimentality in this heartrending story. "Play the facts, just play the facts," he advised this young man who'd never been in front of a camera before. Cautioning Eric against overacting mistakes like too much crying, Duvall quoted one of Sanford Meisner's favorite sayings: "If acting means tears, then my Aunt Tillie is Eleanora Duse."

Eric Fryer was terribly impressed with Duvall, the man as well as the actor. "He's a powerful man, physically and mentally. He throws a football as far as anybody I know, and he conveys enormous authority offscreen as well as on." When the shooting was complete, Duvall gave Fryer a fishing rod as a farewell present, gaining lasting respect for his kindness and generosity and for the power and sensitivity of his performance.

Eric Fryer must have struck a highly responsive chord in Robert Duvall, for whom athletic accomplishments have always been important. Like Terry Fox, Fryer was using his physical prowess to overcome an awesome handicap. Duvall, who takes his sports seriously, had some sense of the kind of endurance these valiant young Canadians had to summon up. While he enjoys spectator sports and knows quite a lot about pro football, it's the participatory sports Duvall thrives on: horseback riding, playing touch football at Adult Day Camp, and boxing.

And, of course, there's his favorite game—tennis. He's awfully good, good enough to have beaten pro football's Jim Brown in a 1971 match that remains one of the highlights of his life. Duvall practices his game six days a week when he's in New York and seven when he's on the Coast, year in and year out except when he's on a remote location and there's no court in sight. The line between hobby and avocation gets fuzzy with extremely intense individuals, and Duvall takes his tennis as seriously as he takes his acting— well, almost.

"If I had my life to do over again, I'd be either a T-formation quarterback—or Caruso. One or the other—or both," this sports-mad amateur musician once said. The sportsman in Duvall is familiar to anyone who's ever watched him play touch football with his friends, spar in the boxing ring, or ride a galloping horse. And the musical side is quickly apparent to anyone who spends a sociable evening in his company because the guitar is never far from his side and there's usually a song pouring out of him.

That musician inside the actor was introduced to the moviegoing public with the release of *Tender Mercies*. It had taken the Hobels a long time to find a distributor, a situation with which Duvall was all too familiar, given his experiences with *Angelo, My Love*. For a while Duvall doubted if *Tender Mercies* would ever see the light of day, but he was too involved with making sure his own film did to directly participate in the Hobels' efforts. These finally did pay off, and Universal agreed to distribute *Tender Mercies*. There was no clumsy mishandling of the initial release as there had been with *The Great Santini*. Suspecting they were dealing with a sleeper, Universal released it slowly, starting in March 1983 in select movie theaters. The following month *Angelo, My Love* was released, so that spring there were two Duvall films showing—one in which he starred, the other that he had produced, written, and directed.

These almost simultaneous openings attracted a great deal of attention to the publicity-shy actor. Serious film criticism articles appeared that drew the parallels between the almost forgotten Boo Radley, the hardly-known Jackson Fentry, and the current Mac Sledge.

Duvall's relationship with the press has always been ambiguous. Jealously guarding his privacy, he's turned down interviews other actors would kill for. But occasionally he would hit it off with a journalist and make some astonishingly frank statements in the course of a routine interview. Always a maverick, his response to publicity is unpredictable. He once startled all who knew of his media reticence by agreeing to pose in an advertisement for a leather fly-boy jacket in the October 1981 issue of *Gentlemen's Quarterly* simply because he liked leather jackets and admired the work of the photographer, Gary Bernstein. His accessibility and avoidance of media coverage have never seemed to follow a calculated or even a particularly logical pattern.

In the interest of promoting both films playing that spring, though, Duvall did give several interviews. As in the past, journalists' impressions of him varied immensely. Some found him taciturn and rather colorless; others had difficulty eliciting enough response from him. Certain interviewers theorized from their own contact with him that Robert Duvall lacks a strong personality of his own, and that this is one of the reasons why he's able to become the characters he plays so totally. Others have been struck by the man's enormous personal charm and his thoroughly unpretentious style. This variety of journalistic reaction probably stems from the fact that Duvall is a man of strong immediate likes and dislikes. With those interviewers who don't strike a responsive chord in him, he can be reticent and remote; with those who do, he can be fascinating.

"Five minutes into lunch with Robert Duvall and I see why he's the most powerful character actor we have. This genial diamond-in-the-rough consumes people's quirks, tics, scraps of conversation, and histories with a voraciousness others reserve for sex or Hershey's Gold Almond bars," rhapsodized a *Vogue* interviewer upon whom the full force of Duvallian charm had obviously been turned.

One of the few journalists to penetrate the wall of privacy Duvall keeps around him was the late Arthur Bell, the clever and urbane columnist for New York's successful antiestablishment weekly *The Village Voice*—hardly a type one would expect Duvall to befriend. But then he has always been unpredictable where the press is concerned. It was Bell who had attended the party for family and friends following the screening of *We're Not the Jet Set* in 1977, and it was Bell who in June 1983, in the full flush of the twin exposure Duvall was enjoying with the simultaneously run-

ning *Angelo, My Love* and *Tender Mercies,* had dinner with the
actor at Eleanora's, Duvall's favorite Italian restaurant in
New York.

In his *Village Voice* column Bell described the meal with
his customary gossipy gusto. It was like eating with Bogart
at Rick's in *Casablanca,* he quipped, with the waiter stopping
in his tracks to show Duvall the fettucine Bolognese, the bus
boy asking him how he liked the prosciutto, and the pro-
prietor, Joseph Lyttle, handing the actor a gallon can of
tomatoes.

"No tomatoes for me, just a salad and a bowl of
minestrone," Duvall said, showing admirable restraint since
pasta with seafood or garlic sauce ranks with crab cakes as
his all-time favorite food.

"Tomorrow, for the party, I'll send over tomatoes,
Bobby," Lyttle assured Duvall.

The party was a family-style gathering for those who had
worked on *Tender Mercies.* It was originally planned by Universal, which wanted to throw a bash at Studio 54. Not the
right atmosphere, Duvall insisted. Instead, he suggested a
thematic hoedown at one of the city's country and western
clubs. Universal nixed that one, calling it too specialized and
too expensive. So Duvall, with characteristic independence,
told the studio to forget the whole thing. He'd throw his
own party at his apartment, just family, friends, crew, and
cast—no public relations flacks, press agents, or columnists.
But Bell did get an invitation, and in his article about the
dinner at Eleanora's also described the party the following
night, giving the public a rare glimpse of the Duvalls at
home.

It was an exuberant gathering, with most of the cooking
done down-home style by Wilford Brimley, who'd flown in
from Tennessee to cook up a storm of country favorites.
Everybody sings at a Bobby Duvall party, from Allan Hub-

bard, who had learned to play the guitar on the set of *Tender Mercies,* to Willie Nelson, a recent acquaintance and old fan of Robert Duvall's. Willie was full of praise for the film, telling Duvall that he looked like Merle Haggard when he was playing Mac Sledge.

"These people Bobby portrayed in his movie, I grew up in those parts and know each of them personally," Willie explained, "and I'll probably be that character he plays some day if I don't take care of myself," he joked.

The famous singer was in good form at Duvall's party, and his music was infectious enough for his host to pick up his guitar and play some duets with him. Arthur Bell, seasoned observer of human nature that he was, said of Duvall playing those duets with Willie Nelson: "He can't control his joy; it's like this is one of the great evenings of his life, the culmination of everything he's worked for. There's a beatific glow on his face."

As well there should be, because Duvall is in his prime and at the peak of his career and enjoying the delights of a happy marriage. When Willie Nelson left, the party moved over to the piano, on which Gail sat as she sang "Since I Fell for You." Coming from a musical family, Gail loves opera as much as her husband and his brothers do and is as eclectic in her musical tastes as they are. Her own talents run to torch songs, and she's pretty good at renditions of white blues numbers. Then it was Jack Duvall's turn. Putting his hand over his heart with a flourish, Bobby's younger brother, lawyer, and agent gave his version of "Danny Boy" as the two giant white doves the Duvalls keep in a cage in the empty fireplace began to coo their accompaniment.

The party didn't break up until after 3 A.M., and its closing was as joyful and special as the rest of it had been. As the guests were starting to fade, Duvall got them all into a circle and, looking like he was "feeling drunk with life," as Bell put it, led his guests in "Amazing Grace."

"Amazing grace, how sweet the sound that saved a wretch like me . . ." the assembled group sang from their collective heart. Then Duvall's voice was heard to soar above the rest—"I once was lost, but now am found, was blind but now I see"—savoring this lavish bestowal of tender mercies on his life.

At the core of Duvall's newfound peace and joy is his love for Gail. For her, he's undergone a fudamental change in his attitudes about the roles of men and women. An interviewer once asked him if he was aware that he had a reputation for being a male chauvinist.

His thoughtful and honest reply was a reflection of his feelings for his new wife: "I'm a conservative guy, and maybe I do have double standards, but I don't think any more so than a lot of people. I have contradictions in myself, but at least I'll speak out if something bothers me. And I've been around bossy women all my life, so I don't like it if someone tries to put me on the spot. I always tend to pick the wrong woman, except for Gail. With somebody like her, I feel at home. Initially, I didn't like the fact that she's an actress. I mean, the competitiveness makes it tough. But I finally said, 'Okay, go ahead.' I used to think a woman should stay home instead of go out and work, but now I think she can do both. I guess in this day and age, it's good that we're trying to understand the grays between the black and white of things."

Not only was Duvall willing to accept Gail's being an actress—he even gave her a push in that direction by making a movie with her. In the summer of 1983 following that exuberant springtime, which had seen so much critical acclaim awarded to both *Angelo, My Love* and *Tender Mercies*,

Duvall made two movies. One was *The Natural,* the baseball fantasy picture starring Robert Redford in which Duvall played the small but memorable part of the hard-boiled sportswriter.

The other movie was a much more modest production, and, therefore, much more in tune with Duvall's style. Duvall got involved with it when he read Gina Berriault's screenplay and took an immediate liking to the character of Joe Hillerman in *The Stone Boy.* The story has been called a rural version of *Ordinary People* because both films tell the story of a family dealing with the tragedy of the accidental death of a son caused by his younger brother. But while the characters in *Ordinary People* were affluent suburbanites availing themselves of the services of a psychiatrist, the family in *The Stone Boy* are Montana farmers. Joe Hillerman is a northwestern version of Duvall's inarticulate, taciturn, decent Southerners.

Duvall was very helpful with the casting, knowing how good Wilford Brimley would be as the grandfather, Glenn Close as the mother, and Freddie Forrest—like Brimley, a friend of the Duvalls—as the brother-in-law. Gail's part was very small at first, but when director Chris Cain saw how fine she was in it, he upgraded the role. Gail plays Lu Jansen, Forrest's estranged wife.

They made the movie the Duvall way, in twenty-one days for $2 million in Great Falls, Montana. That shoestring budget and hard-driving pace have always been his element, as was the magnificant Montana landscape. Except for a few hours of escape to go fly-fishing for trout on the Smith River, it was work all the time, with Duvall loving every moment of it, especially seeing the way Gail took to her role. She said later that her portrayal of Lu came out of some dark recesses in herself.

Her sincerity in the role came across when the picture was

released in April 1984 to mixed reviews, the critics feeling
that most of the cast, Duvall included, weren't given enough
to work with, but that the picture did have an authentic and
moving quality. Some critics, particularly Rex Reed, went on
to single Gail out for special praise.

Rex Reed called hers the best performance: "a stunning
actress with an impressive range. . . . The way she changes
from shy, neurotic, country wife to jazzed up as a cocktail
party waitress with a trashy new lease on life gives the film
its only punch."

With his strongly competitive streak, Duvall might have
resented his wife's besting him in the reviews, but when it
comes to Gail Youngs Duvall, Bobby Duvall is a much more
mellow man than he has ever been before. Because he has
never used tobacco, alcohol, or any other drug, this highly
intense man has had none of the usual releases for tension.
Sometimes in conversation the words tumble out of him
with such a rapidity that he seems to be "speeding on nervous energy," as Arthur Bell once put it. His temperament
has had its abrasive side, to which many directors in Hollywood can attest. But Gail has soothed his nerves, providing
the serene home life he needed to cope with the stresses of
his professional one. He referred to her on a talk show as
"my second and last wife," and calls their marriage "a reality
trip."

In an unusually personal conversation with Arthur Bell,
Duvall spoke of his feelings for his wife: "Of all the women
I've ever known, Gail is the only one I've ever loved. She
can be opinionated, but she's very fair with people. I'm not
a liberal, but she is and she gets real mad if I curse at
strangers or make racial remarks. She has a beautiful soul."

If Gail was the primary cause of the mellowing of Bobby
Duvall, a recognition of a kind he'd never known before
wasn't hurting either. An unusually autonomous man, he

was used to having his own evaluation be the measure of the success of his performances. But now he was being feted in a way entirely new to him and found that this type of attention didn't disagree with him as much as he would have thought; in fact, it was downright gratifying.

In September 1983 Duvall returned to Toronto, exactly a year after making *The Terry Fox Story,* for that city's ambitious eight-year-old film festival. And that year the special tribute was to be for none other than Robert Duvall. He arrived in the city of which he had so many warm memories from his last trip there, with Gail and Jack and his stepdaughter Nancy in tow, not knowing what to expect. All that he had been told was that the Chicago film critics Roger Ebert and Gene Siskel would be hosting the salute to Robert Duvall. What he didn't know was that it was to be an evening out of "This Is Your Life." Duvall stood on the stage with the hosts, facing the glittering audience, uncertain of what was happening next.

What happened was that Horton Foote and his wife, Lillian, walked onto the stage; then Ulu Grosbard and Rose Gregorio. Then came the biggest surprise of all—straight from the set of his latest extravagant epic, *The Cotton Club,* and larger-than-life as ever, was Francis Coppola, who had flown up in a chartered plane with his wife.

The hosts showed clippings of Duvall in movies he'd made over two decades from *To Kill a Mockingbird* to *Tender Mercies,* and many of the richly varied roles in between Boo Radley and Mac Sledge. The clippings alone would have been a tribute in themselves, but there were speeches and anecdotes, and the air was thick with the warmth of the feeling his old friends had for the maverick actor with more than a touch of genius.

As he always does, Coppola tended to tower over everyone else, dominating the occasion by the power of his presence. He told stories about Duvall on the set of *The Godfather*, about how he had imitated Brando whenever the star's back was turned. Then it was Duvall's turn to remind Coppola of those days when Paramount's Bob Evans had had an understudy director following Coppola around on *The Godfather* set so that he could fire him any time he chose to. Of course everyone was aware that, with typical moviemaking irony, it was Bob Evans who was producing the latest Coppola opus.

Duvall couldn't resist reminding Coppola of that scene cut from *Apocalypse Now;* his tone was appropriately light, but underneath it the old hurt and indignation were still there.

"I suspected your liberal friends in San Francisco talked you into getting rid of that," Duvall chided.

Coppola then launched into an explanation about how overly long the film was and how much cutting it needed, finishing off this rather lame apology with: "That's one scene I wished we'd left in." But his audience seemed as skeptical at that statement as did Duvall.

Despite the hurtful old memory, it was a wonderful evening full of fun and the praise that flows like champagne at film festivals. With the Footes and the Grosbards and the Coppolas, his brother, his wife, and his stepdaughter, Robert Duvall was able to savor a welcome sense of security and continuity.

Another kind of continuity came to an end a few months later in the winter of 1984 when Rear Admiral William Howard Duvall died in Alexandria. He had lived to a ripe old age, and he and Mildred had spent the last few years in a retirement home, retaining their good spirits and sociability and their love of music and family reunions to the end.

Grieving, Robert Duvall could take comfort in the fact

that his father had lived to see his middle son gain such widespread recognition in the profession he had had the foresight to guide him toward. The path Bodge had embarked upon in college had led a long way from Elsah, Illinois, and he had enjoyed his family's moral support every step of the way.

Now that path was leading to the greatest honor Hollywood can bestow—the Academy Awards. The awards were nothing new to Duvall, who had been nominated twice for supporting actor for his roles in *The Godfather* and *Apocalypse Now,* and once for Best Actor for *The Great Santini,* which he'd lost to Robert De Niro for his performance in *Raging Bull.* The glittering prizes had never held much charm for Duvall, but the Oscar was a symbol of a recognition he knew was much deserved, and he did want it—not desperately, but probably more than he let anybody know.

In April 1984, inside the packed Dorothy Chandler Pavilion in Hollywood, Ms. Country herself, Dolly Parton, shouted out the name "Robert Duvall" as winner of the Best Actor Award for his portrayal of Mac Sledge in *Tender Mercies.* The crowd let out a roar of appreciation for this man who had brought so many unforgettable characters to the screen that he'd almost been forgotten himself in the process. "It was a nice feeling," Duvall admitted, "knowing I was the home-crowd favorite."

There was another triumph that night when Horton Foote won the Oscar for the Best Original Screenplay. A twin triumph, actually, for these two superbly creative men who for two decades had shared a vision of rendering a way of life, the essence of a vastly misunderstood region of the United States, on film, depicting its people as they really are without the usual cheapening distortions.

From the unknown playwright who'd come to the Neighborhood Playhouse to watch a drama class put on a performance of his television one-acter, "The Midnight Caller," and the young student who'd sobbed as though his heart were breaking as the play's anguished hero, Horton Foote and Robert Duvall had come a long way. It was Foote who opened the Hollywood door for Duvall with *To Kill a Mockingbird,* and it was with Foote that Duvall had shared the artistic excitement of making *Tomorrow,* and then the subsequent disappointment that the film wasn't better received.

In *Tender Mercies,* these two veterans of struggles for creative control of films in which they were involved finally had all the right elements going for them. And the result was the glittering statuette each held in his hand on that gala occasion, symbol of a sweet victory for their style of moviemaking and for their dedication to holding out for that which is best.

The aftermath of the Academy Awards was a typical Duvall scenario. When he found he couldn't get all his country friends into the grand post-Oscar ball, he left the event, his only regret being the food he would be missing. "I love rack of lamb intensely," he sighed. Then he took his down-home entourage over to Johnny Cash's bungalow, where they devoured batches of hamburgers.

Country music, country people, and country customs were dominating Duvall's thoughts more and more. In an interview he gave for *People* magazine just after his Academy Award he spoke with a rush of feeling about Southerners: "I love those people, I can't learn enough from them. Southerners, Texans, cowboys and country singers, the sort of folks you see all lean as leather out there in the southwest or up along the Rocky Mountains. How tough and vengeful and loving they are, how serious and religious in the best sense of the word. Part of it is the mystery at the heart of Fundamentalism. It's the link that was struck in the

South, at least between the whites and the blacks. You don't see that in the North. My father was a Virginian—born and raised in Lorton, near Alexandria—and way back, in the early 1800's there was French Huguenot in the background. A fellow named Maureen Duvall. A *man* named Maureen! We had ancestors who fought on both sides in the Civil War. Maybe that's where my fascination with those kinds of people comes from."

That mystery at the heart of Fundamentalism was increasingly on his mind, a new character taking shape in his head and in his heart. Preachers had always fascinated him, and he'd incorporated a bit of the Pentecostal into his innovative interpretation of Jesse James in *The Great Northfield Minnesota Raid*. In the post-Oscar glow of success, Duvall turned his energies toward this new image and wrote a screenplay about a guilt-wracked evangelical preacher. He wants to produce the film and to star in it, a first for Duvall, who has written his own scripts before but has never starred in a movie he has written and produced himself. He wants Richard Pearce to direct this new work, entitled *The Apostle.* Pearce was the director of *Heartland,* a low-budget movie about life on the northwestern frontier in the last century, a film unique for its realism and harsh beauty. Pearce is one of the few directors who should be able to live up to Duvall's standards for authenticity and integrity.

The new picture has an upbeat theme and deals squarely with controversial issues, even going so far as to have the preacher nailed for tax evasion and imprisoned by the IRS. Duvall wants Johnny Cash to write the music for it. He and Cash have already put out a country single together. It's called "The Orchid Is a Flower," though Duvall always calls it "I Overlooked an Orchid While Searching for a Rose." "I heard a blind guy sing it in New York twenty-five years ago and I was going to sing it in *Nashville* when I thought I was going to be in the movie. With Johnny, I sang the second verse wrong, but he liked it that way and didn't tell me," Duvall explained.

Duvall liked that recording experience so much that he went down to Nashville and cut an album of country music with Johnny Cash, getting plenty of help from the likes of June Carter Cash, Willie Nelson, and Waylon Jennings. The album, which has yet to be released, may well be the start of an entirely new phase to the extraordinary Duvall career. Since *Tender Mercies* he's gained the respect and friendship of the big country and western stars he's so long admired and may very well become seriously involved with country music.

Duvall's future prospects remain as varied as his acting career has been so far. After the film about the pentecostal preacher, he may have completed his cycle of explorations into the heart and mind of the American Southland, or there may be a lot more to be said on that subject.

Now that he's won an Oscar, will he accept only lead roles? Probably not. Duvall has always been attracted to the substance of a part rather than its star potential, and that's unlikely to change with his recent success. He'll never be a "star," and whether he has the lead or the supporting role, he'll always see it as a character part, a character in whose memories he'll hang around until he has him down as no one else ever could.

His career will undoubtedly continue to be as multi-faceted as it has been these last several years. He has honed his skills as a producer, director, and screenplay writer, and now he can choose any combination of these for work on a new project. He can write, produce, and direct another film as he did with *Angelo, My Love;* or he can find a new subject suitable for a documentary and make another film like *We're Not the Jet Set;* or he can pursue his interest in writing, acting, and producing and leave the directing to someone else, as he is doing on *The Apostle*.

Then there is always the Broadway stage, to which he is likely to return at more frequent intervals now that his financial situation can allow him to sustain the monetary loss a movie actor almost always has to withstand on the far less lucrative stage. Whether it's Broadway or Hollywood, he's sure to be working with Horton Foote and Ulu Grosbard again. These are connections forged over half a lifetime, and whenever he can Duvall will avail himself of his old friends' and colleagues' considerable talents.

There may be more movies with Gail coming up. In *The Stone Boy* she showed the signs of being a truly talented actress, and there's every reason to believe that her husband will help her to develop this ability. Now that he's finally overcome his aversion to the concept of the working wife, Duvall is likely to take on the informal management of Gail's career with all his usual thoroughness and intensity.

For Duvall, though, whoever his director or costars, whatever the circumstances of the film, it will always come down to the part itself. The role must tug at him, wrap itself around his consciousness so that he just has to play it. It's as though certain roles call out to him to play them and he has no choice but to comply.

One possible future role was suggested to him when he read *Schindler's List* by Thomas Keneally, a book about the German industrialist who risked his life as well as his fortune to save more than a thousand Jews during World War II. Talking about Oskar Schindler, speculating on what kind of a man he must have been, Duvall urgently says, "I must play this part." There has also been talk of his playing the pope in a movie called *Saving Grace,* which contains a part for Angelo Evans. He never stops turning over new ideas in his head, trying on new parts for size to see which fits perfectly.

"If you don't daydream and kind of plan things out in your imagination, you never get there," Duvall says. "So you have to start someplace."

Actors like Robert Duvall never rest on their laurels because that's not their nature. They keep searching for new challenges. It can't be easy, but it won't be boring, either. There are still the commercial considerations that can't be put aside. *Tender Mercies,* for all its critical appeal and motion-picture industry recognition, didn't do well at the box office. Then, when it went on HBO in March 1984, a year after its movie theater release, it topped the three major networks on the ratings for homes with cable TV.

There's a revolution in the movie industry brought about first by cable TV and now by video cassettes. Duvall's movies have never done that well at the box office; they may do much better in the living room. While he is no longer in the position of having to make movies he doesn't want to because he needs the money, he still needs to make movies that will make him money.

It is unlikely that America's Olivier will turn to the classics on either stage or screen. Eddie Carbone was his Othello, Jackson Fentry his Lear. It's modern man with all his contradictions and complexities that Duvall wants to capture in his characterizations. Now that he is in a position to have more say about scripts and more control over directors, there will be more of those contradictions in his parts. The good guys will have more malice in them, and the bad ones more flashes of nobility. The subtle interplay of self-interest and altruism in human motivation will be given a wider range of expression in future Duvall parts.

While it's not likely that Duvall will play Shakespeare, it's virtually impossible to imagine him in a drawing room comedy part, whether in Hollywood or on Broadway. Because he's not interested in frivolity or fashion, he will be partial to those roles where the characters, however inarticulate, possess great depths of emotion. And he will care only to portray people who have about them the unmistakable feel of reality. His characters, though their backgrounds and circumstances may be atypical, will always be recognizable as authentic human types, never as reflections of Hollywood's deplorable tendencies to glamorize that which is austere and to simplify that which is complex.

Although he will never play a frivolous part, that doesn't mean Duvall won't develop his talent for comedy. With his cops and his cowboys, his soldiers and desperados, he hasn't yet been given the opportunity to demonstrate his affinity for humor. He was very funny as Frank Burns in *M*A*S*H* and, in a more subtle mode, there was humor in his depiction of the ruthless TV executive in *Network*. But both of those roles were ones in which he was called upon to show his admirable restraint, holding back on the force of his performance so that it didn't detract from the films' leading roles. Then, when the restraints were removed in *Apocalypse Now*, his portrayal of Colonel Kilgore demonstrated an absolutely brilliant comic sense.

Good comedy is hard to come by. Duvall will always steer clear of the slapstick as emphatically as he will the lightweight. What he needs are more roles like Kilgore and Bull Meechum, in which he enacts the funny side of menacing characters. Meechum clowning it up is hilarious; a whole new dimension is added to that multifaceted man who can be in turn courageous, contemptible, and pathetic. Kilgore was as funny in those satirical scenes as he was frightening in his exuberant fanaticism. For an actor whose career has been largely one of character roles, Duvall has had far too few ones with comic components. If he can find more of them, a new dimension to his own acting may well emerge.

It has been said of Duvall's characterizations that "he looks for the tiniest tear in society's fabric." That's because he is fascinated with people who are marginal, who live on the jagged edge of the plastic, homogenized culture. Whether he is playing a dirt farmer, a Marine flyer, a cynical detective, or a country singer, Duvall is drawn to the man who is alienated from the larger society that has in one way or another rejected him.

In one sense those marginal men he plays are a reflection of Robert Duvall—not that he has ever been rejected by society. But he has rejected a part of it. From the beginning of his career he has rejected the calculated hype and the contrived façade that have been considered the necessities of making it as an actor. People at the margins of their professions often anticipate trends. By the way he has conducted his career, Duvall has unknowingly helped to create a new kind of actor.

This new breed is apparent in that group of actors several years younger than Duvall who have refused the social role of movie star—men like Dustin Hoffman, Robert De Niro, and Al Pacino. Like Duvall, they underwent a grueling apprenticeship, and, like him, their energies are focused on the parts they are playing, not on the personal images they are projecting. Duvall, who has been painstakingly building his repertoire of roles and, at the same time, zealously guarding the privacy of his personal life, may well be the prototype not only for the current crop of ambitious actors, but also for future generations of talented young men striving for recognition on screen and stage.

The age of glittering movie stars is a thing of the past. With its old rival, television, and its new one spawned by the video revolution, the Hollywood studio is in no position to be grinding out new names and faces pasted onto the old and tarnished images of stars inhabiting another world from the real one of their avid fans.

In this new era those actors and actresses with the most flexibility and the least concern with status and labels will have the best chance of making it. Feature films, major network TV movies, pictures made for cable TV, and eventually, perhaps, pictures produced solely for VCR distribution—the actor of the future will have to be at home in this highly diversified milieu of motion picture production. The potential roles will be equally diversified. As the old image of the movie star fades, the categories of roles may become more fluid and the ability of an actor to shift comfortably among leading, featuring, and character parts will become increasingly more important.

In such a climate Duvall's career path and personal style could provide a guideline for aspiring actors. Today's maverick often becomes tomorrow's role model. And no career can better serve as an ideal to be respected and emulated than Robert Duvall's, brimming as always with diversification, integrity, and an amazing talent.

ROBERT DUVALL's CAREER

Films

TO KILL A MOCKINGBIRD
1963
Written by: Horton Foote
Directed by: Robert Mulligan
Distributed by: Universal
  Pictures
Produced by: Alan J. Pakula
Starring: Gregory Peck, Mary
  Badham

CAPTAIN NEWMAN, M.D.
1964
Written by: Richard L. Breen
  & Phoebe & Henry Ephron
Directed by: David Miller
Distributed by: Universal
  Pictures
Produced by: Robert Arthur
Starring: Gregory Peck, Tony
  Curtis, Bobby Darin, Eddie
  Albert, Angie Dickinson

THE CHASE
1964
Written by: Lillian Hellman
Directed by: Arthur Penn
Photography by: Joseph La
  Shelle
Music by: John Barry
Distributed by: Columbia
  Pictures

Produced by: Sam Spiegel
Starring: Marlon Brando,
  Jane Fonda, Robert Redford,
  Angie Dickinson, E. G.
  Marshall, Janice Rule

COUNTDOWN
1968
Written by: Loring Mandel
Directed by: Robert Altman
Distributed by: Warner
  Brothers–Seven Arts
Produced by: William Conrad
Starring: James Caan, Joanna
  Moore

THE DETECTIVE
1968
Written by: Abby Mann
Directed by: Gordon Douglas
Distributed by: 20th
  Century–Fox
Produced by: Aaron
  Rosenberg
Starring: Frank Sinatra, Lee
  Remick

BULLITT
1968
Written by: Alan R. Trustman

Directed by: Peter Yates
Distributed by: Warner
  Brothers–Seven Arts
Produced by: Philip D'Antoni
Starring: Steve McQueen,
  Jacqueline Bisset

TRUE GRIT
1969
Written by: Marguerite
  Roberts
Directed by: Henry Hathaway
Distributed by: Paramount
  Pictures
Produced by: Hal Wallis
Starring: John Wayne, Glen
  Campbell

THE RAIN PEOPLE
1969
Written & Directed by:
  Francis Coppola
Distributed by: Warner
  Brothers–Seven Arts
Produced by: Bart Patton &
  Ronald Colby
Starring: James Caan, Shirley
  Knight

M*A*S*H
1970
Written by: Ring Lardner, Jr.
Directed by: Robert Altman
Photography by: Harold E.
  Stine
Music by: Johnny Mandel

Distributed by: 20th Century–
  Fox
Produced by: Ingo Preminger
Starring: Elliott Gould,
  Donald Sutherland, Sally
  Kellerman

THE REVOLUTIONARY
1970
Written by: Hans
  Koenigsberger
Directed by: Paul Williams
Music by: Mike Small
Distributed by: United Artists
Produced by: Edward
  Rambach Pressman
Starring: Jon Voight, Jennifer
  Salt

THX-1138
1971
Written by: George Lucas &
  Walter Murch
Directed by: George Lucas
Photography by: Dave Meyers
  & Albert Kihn
Music by: Lalo Schifrin
Distributed by: Warner
  Brothers
Produced by: Lawrence
  Sturhan
Starring: Donald Pleasance,
  Maggie McOmie

LAWMAN
1971
Written by: Gerald Wilson
Directed & Produced by:
  Michael Winner
Music by: Jerry Fielding
Distributed by: United Artists
Starring: Burt Lancaster,
  Robert Ryan, Lee J. Cobb

THE GODFATHER
1972
Written by: Mario Puzo &
  Francis Coppola
Directed by: Francis Coppola
Photography by: Gordon
  Willis
Music by: Nino Rota
Distributed by: Paramount
  Pictures
Produced by: Albert S. Ruddy
Starring: Marlon Brando, Al
  Pacino, James Caan

TOMORROW
1972
Written by: Horton Foote
Directed by: Joseph Anthony
Photography by: Allan Green
Music by: Irwin Stahl
Distributed by: Film Group
  Production
Produced by: Gilbert
  Pearlman & Paul Roebling
Starring: Olga Bellin

**THE GREAT
NORTHFIELD
MINNESOTA RAID**
1972
Written & Directed by: Philip
  Kaufman
Photography by: Bruce
  Surtees
Music by: Dave Grusin
Distributed by: Universal
  Pictures
Produced by: Jennings Lang
Starring: Cliff Robertson,
  Luke Askew

JOE KIDD
1972
Written by: Elmore Leonard
Directed by: John Sturges
Photography by: Bruce
  Surtees
Music by: Lalo Schifrin
Distributed by: Universal
Produced by: Robert Daley &
  Sidney Beckerman
Starring: Clint Eastwood

LADY ICE
1973
Written by: Alan Trustman &
  Harold Clemens
Directed by: Tom Gries
Photography by: Lucien
  Ballard
Music by: Perry Botkin, Jr.

Distributed by: National
General Pictures
Produced by: Harrison Starr
Starring: Donald Sutherland,
Jennifer O'Neill

BADGE 373
1973
Written by: Pete Hamill
Directed by: Howard W. Koch
Photography by: Arthur
Ornitz
Music by: J. J. Jackson
Distributed by: Paramount
Pictures
Starring: Verna Bloom, Eddie
Egan

THE OUTFIT
1974
Written and Directed by:
John Flynn
Photography by: Bruce
Surtees
Music by: Jerry Fielding
Distributed by: United Artists
Produced by: Carter De
Haven
Starring: Karen Black, Robert
Ryan

THE CONVERSATION
1974
Written and Directed by:
Francis Coppola
Photography by: Bill Butler

Music by: David Shire
Distributed by: Paramount
Pictures
Produced by: Fred Roos
Starring: Gene Hackman,
John Cazale

THE GODFATHER, PART II
1974
Written by: Francis Coppola
& Mario Puzo
Directed & Produced by:
Francis Coppola
Photography by: Gordon
Willis
Music by: Nino Rota
Distributed by: Paramount
Pictures
Starring: Al Pacino, Diane
Keaton, Robert De Niro, Lee
Strasberg

BREAKOUT
1975
Written by: Howard B.
Kreitsek
Directed by: Tom Gries
Photography by: Lucien
Ballard
Music by: Jerry Goldsmith
Distributed by: Columbia
Pictures
Produced by: Robert Chartoff
& Irwin Winkler
Starring: Charles Bronson, Jill
Ireland, John Huston

THE KILLER ELITE
1975
Written by: Stirling Silliphant
Directed by: Sam Peckinpah
Photography by: Phil Lathrop
Distributed by: United Artists
Produced by: Martin Baum &
  Arthur Lewis
Starring: James Caan, Arthur
  Hill, Gig Young

NETWORK
1976
Written by: Paddy Chayefsky
Directed by: Sidney Lumet
Photography by: Owen
  Roizman
Music by: Elliot Lawrence
Distributed by: United Artists
Produced by: Howard
  Gottfried
Starring: Faye Dunaway,
  William Holden, Peter Finch

**THE SEVEN-PER-CENT
SOLUTION**
1976
Written by: Nicholas Meyer
Directed by: Herbert Ross
Photography by: Oswald
  Morris
Music by: John Addison
Distributed by: Universal
  Pictures
Produced by: Herbert Ross
Starring: Nicol Williamson,

Alan Arkin, Laurence
Olivier, Vanessa Redgrave

THE EAGLE HAS LANDED
1977
Written by: Tom Mankiewicz
Directed by: John Sturges
Photography by: Anthony
  Richmond
Music by: Lalo Schifrin
Distributed by: Columbia
  Pictures
Produced by: Jack Wiener &
  David Niven, Jr.
Starring: Michael Caine,
  Donald Sutherland, Donald
  Pleasance

THE GREATEST
1977
Written by: Ring Lardner, Jr.
Directed by: Tom Gries
Photography by: Harry
  Stradling, Jr.
Music by: Michael Masser
Distributed by: Columbia
  Pictures
Produced by: John Marshall
Starring: Muhammad Ali,
  Ernest Borgnine, James Earl
  Jones

THE BETSY
1978
Written by: Walter Bernstein
  & William Bast

Directed by: Daniel Petrie
Photography by: Mario Tosi
Music by: John Barry
Distributed by: Allied Artists
  Corporation
Produced by: Robert R.
  Weston
Starring: Laurence Olivier,
  Katharine Ross, Tommy Lee
  Jones, Jane Alexander

APOCALYPSE NOW
1979
Written by: John Milius &
  Francis Coppola
Directed and Produced by:
  Francis Coppola
Photography by: Vittorio
  Storaro
Music by: Carmine Coppola &
  Francis Coppola
Distributed by: United Artists
Starring: Marlon Brando,
  Martin Sheen

THE GREAT SANTINI
1980
Written and Directed by:
  Lewis John Carlino
Photography by: Ralph
  Woolsey
Music by: Elmer Bernstein
Distributed by: Warner
  Communications
Produced by: Charles A. Pratt
Starring: Blythe Danner &
  Michael O'Keefe

TRUE CONFESSIONS
1981
Written by: John Gregory
  Dunne & Joan Didion
Directed by: Ulu Grosbard
Photography by: Owen
  Roizman
Music by: Georges Delerue
Distributed by: United Artists
Produced by: Robert Chartoff
  & Irwin Wrinkler
Starring: Robert De Niro,
  Charles Durning, Burgess
  Meredith, Rose Gregorio

THE PURSUIT OF D. B. COOPER
1981
Written by: Jeffrey Alan
  Fiskin
Directed by: Roger
  Spottiswoode
Photography by: Preston
  Ames
Music by: James Horner &
  Waylon Jennings
Distributed by: Universal
  Pictures
Produced by: Daniel Wigutow
  & Michael Taylor
Starring: Treat Williams,
  Kathryn Harrold,

TENDER MERCIES
1983
Written by: Horton Foote
Directed by: Bruce Beresford

Photography by: Russell Boyd
Music by: Various composers
including Robert Duvall
Distributed by: Universal
Pictures
Produced by: Philip & Mary
Ann Hobel
Starring: Tess Harper, Allan
Hubbard, Betty Buckley,
Ellen Barkin

THE NATURAL
1984
Written by: Roger Towne &
Phil Dusenberry
Directed by: Barry Levinson
Photography by: Caleb
Deschanel
Music by: Randy Newman
Distributed by: Tri Star

Pictures
Produced by: Mark Johnson
Starring: Robert Redford,
Glenn Close, Wilford
Brimley

THE STONE BOY
1984
Written by: Gina Berriault
Directed by: Christopher Cain
Photography by: Juan Ruiz-
Anchia
Music by: Hames Horner
Distributed by: 20th
Century–Fox
Produced by: Joe Roth & Ivan
Block
Starring: Frederic Forrest,
Glenn Close, Wilford
Brimley, Gail Youngs

Plays

CALL ME BY MY RIGHTFUL NAME
1961
Written by: Michael Shurlteff
Directed by: Milton Katselas
Produced by: Judy Rutherford
Starring: Alvin Ailey, Joan Hackett
Presented at: One Sheridan Square Theater

THE DAYS AND NIGHTS OF BEEBEE FENSTERMAKER
1962
Written by: William Snyder
Directed by: Ulu Grosbard
Produced by: Judy Rutherford Marechal & Ulu Grosbard
Starring: Rose Gregorio
Presented at: Sheridan Square Playhouse

A VIEW FROM THE BRIDGE
1965
Written by: Arthur Miller
Directed by: Ulu Grosbard
Produced by: Joseph E. Levine
Starring: Jon Voight, Susan Anspach
Presented at: Sheridan Square Playhouse

WAIT UNTIL DARK
1966
Written by: Frederick Knott
Directed by: Arthur Penn
Produced by: Fred Coe
Starring: Lee Remick
Presented at: Ethel Barrymore Theatre

AMERICAN BUFFALO
1977
Written by: David Mamet
Directed by: Ulu Grosbard
Produced by: Joseph Beruh & Edgar Lansbury
Starring: Kenneth McMillan, John Savage
Presented at: Ethel Barrymore Theatre

TV Films

IKE
1979
Teleplay by: Melville Shavelson

Directed by: Melville
  Shavelson & Boris Sagal
Photography by: Arch R.
  Dalzell & Freddie Young
Music by: Fred Karlin
Presented by: ABC Circle
  Films
Produced by: Melville
  Shavelson & Bill McCutchen
Starring: Lee Remick, Dana
  Andrews

THE TERRY FOX STORY
1983
Written by: John & Rose
  Kastner
Directed by: Ralph Thomas
Photography by: Richard
  Ciupka
Music by: Bill Conti
Distributed by: HBO in the
  U.S. & 20th Century–Fox in
  Canada
Produced by: Robert Cooper
Starring: Eric Fryer

Films directed by Robert Duvall

**WE'RE NOT THE JET SET
(Documentary)**
1977
Directed by: Robert Duvall
Produced by: Barbara Duvall
Photography by: Tony
  Donovan, Tony Foresta &
  Joseph Friedman
Starring: B.A. & Eunice
  Peterson & members of their
  family

**ANGELO, MY LOVE
(Feature Film)**
1983
Written & Directed by: Robert
  Duvall
Photography by: Joseph
  Friedman
Music by: Michael Kamen
Distributed by: Cinecom
  International Films
Produced by: Robert Duvall &
  Gail Youngs
Starring: Angelo Evans &
  members of his family

ABOUT THE AUTHOR

Judith Slawson is a free-lance writer whose articles on current trends and contemporary life-styles have appeared in *Mademoiselle, The New York Times, The Villager* and *The Kingston Daily Freeman.* She makes her home in Greenwich Village and in Woodstock, New York, and is presently at work on her first novel.

INDEX